TREVOR WYE
Complete Daily Exercises for the flute

*For Larry Krantz, Nelson Pardee, John Rayworth and Helen Spielman
for their initiative and dedication to the Internet FLUTE List,
a great tool for the advancement of our knowledge of the flute.*

Novello Publishing Limited

Contents

Preface 4

SECTION 1: TONE EXERCISES, WARM-UPS AND VOCALISE

1 **Extract from Daily Exercise No.2 (Reichert)** 5
2 **Extract from Violin Concerto (Brahms)** 6
3 **Extract from Il Fortuno di Destino (Verdi)** 6
4 **Akatombo (Kosaku Yamada)** 7
5 **Extract from Daily Exercises No.5 (Reichert)** 7
6 **Extract from Flute Concerto (Reinecke)** 8
7 **Extract from Peer Gynt Suite (Grieg)** 8
8 **Extract from La Sensible (Royer)** 9

SECTION 2: SCALES AND SCALE EXERCISES

1 **Major Scales to top B or D** 12
2 **Harmonic Minor Scales to top B or D** 13
3 **Whole Tone Scales** 14
4 **Major Scales to top B or D in thirds** 15
5 **Minor Scales to top B or D in thirds** 17
6 **Broken Whole Tone Scales** 19
   Daily Exercises on Scales:
7 **Major Scale Exercise** 20
8 **Minor Scale Exercise** 22
9 **Major and Minor Scale Exercises** 23
10 **No.1 from Seven Daily Exercises (Reichert)** 28
11 **Cascading Major and Minor Scales** 29

SECTION THREE: ARPEGGIOS

1 **Arpeggios to top B and low C** 33
2 **Extended Arpeggios to top D and low B** 34
3 **Augmented 5th Arpeggios** 35
4 **Diminished 7th Arpeggios** 35
5 **Arpeggios of the 7th** 36
6 **Arpeggio Study 1** 36
7 **Arpeggio Study 2** 38
8 **Daily Exercise No.1 (Maquarre)** 40
9 **Daily Exercise No.5 (Maquarre)** 42
10 **Broken Arpeggios** 46
11 **Broken 7th Arpeggios** 47
12 **Broken Augmented 5th Arpeggios** 48
13 **Broken Diminished 7th Arpeggios** 48
14 **Broken Arpeggio Study** 48
15 **No.2 from Seven Daily Exercises (Reichert)** 52
16 **No.4 from Seven Daily Exercises (Reichert)** 56
17 **No.5 from Seven Daily Exercises (Reichert)** 58
18 **No.7 from Seven Daily Exercises (Reichert)** 62
19 **No.1 from Twelve Studies (Boehm)** 64
20 **No.11 from Twelve Studies (Boehm)** 65

SECTION FOUR: CHROMATIC EXERCISES

1. **Chromatic Scale to top C or D** 67
2. **Broken Chromatic Scales** 67
3. **No. 6 from Seven Daily Exercises (Reichert)** 68
4. **Four Chromatic Sequences** 70
5. **First Chromatic Study** 72
6. **Second Chromatic Study** 73

SECTION FIVE: THE THIRD OCTAVE

**Six exercises from D.S. Wood's *Technical Exercises
for Facilitating the Execution of the Upper Notes of the Flute***

1. **Scales** 74
2. **Broken Scales 1** 78
3. **Broken Scales 2** 81
4. **Thirds 1** 84
5. **Thirds 2** 87
6. **Thirds 3** 90
7. **Chromatic** 93
8. **Final Study** 94

SECTION SIX: DAILY EXERCISES

1. **Daily Exercise No.1 (Wye)** 96
2. **Daily Exercise No.2 (Wye)** 98
3. **Daily Exercise No.3 (Wye)** 100
4. **Daily Exercise No.4 (Wye)** 102
5. **Twelve Studies No.2 (Boehm)** 106
6. **Twelve Studies No.3 (Boehm)** 107
7. **Twelve Studies No.4 (Boehm)** 110
8. **Twelve Studies No.9 (Boehm)** 112
9. **Twelve Studies No.12 (Boehm)** 116
10. **Twelve Studies No.10 (Boehm)** 118
11. **Right and Left Hand Co-ordination Exercise** 121
12. **Four Studies on *Perpetuum Mobile*** 122

Practising 127

Exclusive distributors:
Music Sales Limited, Newmarket Road,
Bury St Edmunds, Suffolk IP33 3YB.

Order No. NOV120850   ISBN 0-85360-935-7
© Copyright 1999 Novello & Company Limited.
Music processed by Barnes Engraving
Cover design by Chloë Alexander

No part of this publication may be copied or reproduced in any form
or by any means without the prior permission of Novello Publishing Limited.

Preface

I have often thought 'If only there was a book containing all of the daily exercises!' Well here it is.

This book contains the traditional exercises which most flautists worldwide use in their daily workout. They were based on the five most popular 'French School' study books, though some of them have been modified in the light of present day practice and custom, but, for those who prefer it the original material is still covered, too.

I have taken the liberty of extending the compass of some of the favourites to top D, or to low B, which is often now required, but allowing those with more traditional views to retain the old format if they wish. In order to save space, I have excluded the less important exercises, and added some new ones of my own – based on old ideas – which I find useful. I also wish to add that most of these exercises are fairly easy to memorise, a skill which is widely recognised as having great benefits for the future of any young player. Learning to memorise can be thought of as an investment, or 'money in the bank'!

Where appropriate, I have suggested ways of practising these exercises based on my experiences in teaching. Of course, there are as many ideas on practising as there are people playing the flute, but I hope you find these hints useful.

Finally, the Practice Card can be moved about the book and referred to for your daily practice scheme. It also provides a guide to different articulation patterns which can be used with most exercises.

Trevor Wye

SECTION 1

Tone Exercises, Warm-ups and 'Vocalise'

Every player has, at some time or another, been captivated by the beauty of a good melody, and used it to help them develop their tone. Moyse developed this idea further by compiling vocal melodies he heard at the Opéra Comique in Paris.

The first of these 'vocalise' by Reichert has been a standard warm-up exercise since the days of Paul Taffanel and perhaps before him. Moyse used this sequence in his classes to help encourage and develop the imagination of his students. It remains my all-time favourite, especially when used with different colours.* It is ideal to begin the day with this simple sequential exercise to warm-up the lips, the breathing, and begin to add expression.

The other exercises were suggested by enthusiastic students over the years. The 'expression' or 'interpretation' used to vocalise these melodies is personal, though I have made a suggestion as to how to start, but to gain the most benefit from them, a lot depends on the way they are played.

Exercise No.8 by Royer is useful for developing the strength of the lips and tone when moving from octave to octave.

As always, these exercises are better committed to memory because of the freedom of expression gained through dispensing with the process of reading the notes.

Blank pages have been added for you to add your own melodies.

1

The full exercise can be found on page 52. As a tone exercise it should be practised in all twenty-four keys, as each key has its own problems of tone, colour and intonation.*

Reichert Daily Exercise No.2

This exercise may also be practised in the following way:

* See Practice Book One TONE, Page 24 – Tone Colour

4

Repeat *p* each time.

'Akatombo' by Kosaku Yamada

Continue in the following keys:

5

See page 56 for the complete exercise in 24 keys. Some days, start in one of the middle keys so that different problems are encountered and overcome.

Repeat *p* each time

Reichert Daily Exercise No.5

6

From Reinecke's Flute Concerto

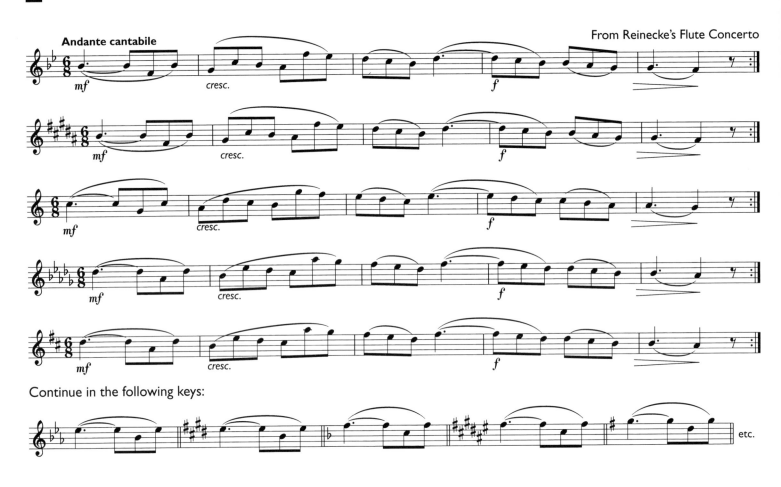

Continue in the following keys:

7

This exercise is good for practising a soft, muted tone colour, and for breath control.
Repeat *p* each time

The Death of Ase
From Grieg's 'Peer Gynt Suite'

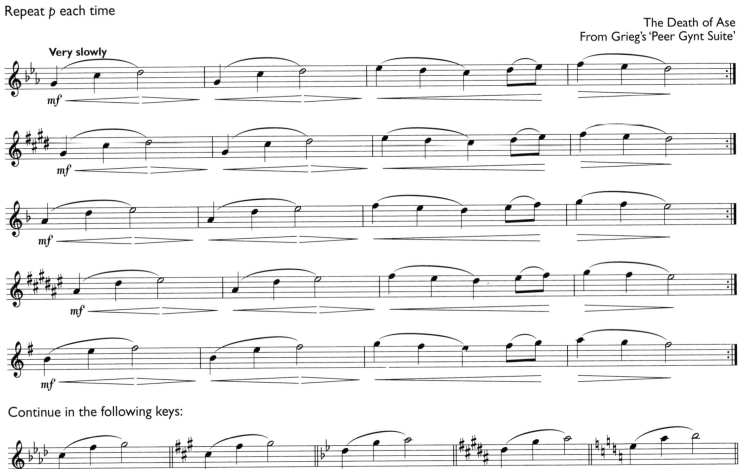

Continue in the following keys:

The Low Register

This exercise can be practised with various nuances and is useful for learning to 'follow' the notes with the embouchure, which helps achieve beauty and evenness of tone when moving through large intervals. If this first exercise is awkward for you to read, then choose an easier key to start with.

8

Repeat *mp*, *p* and *pp* each time

From Royer's 'La Sensible'

The Middle and High Registers
When moving between registers, how easy it is to crack the notes!
Aim for clean and flexible intervals.

Repeat *p* each time.

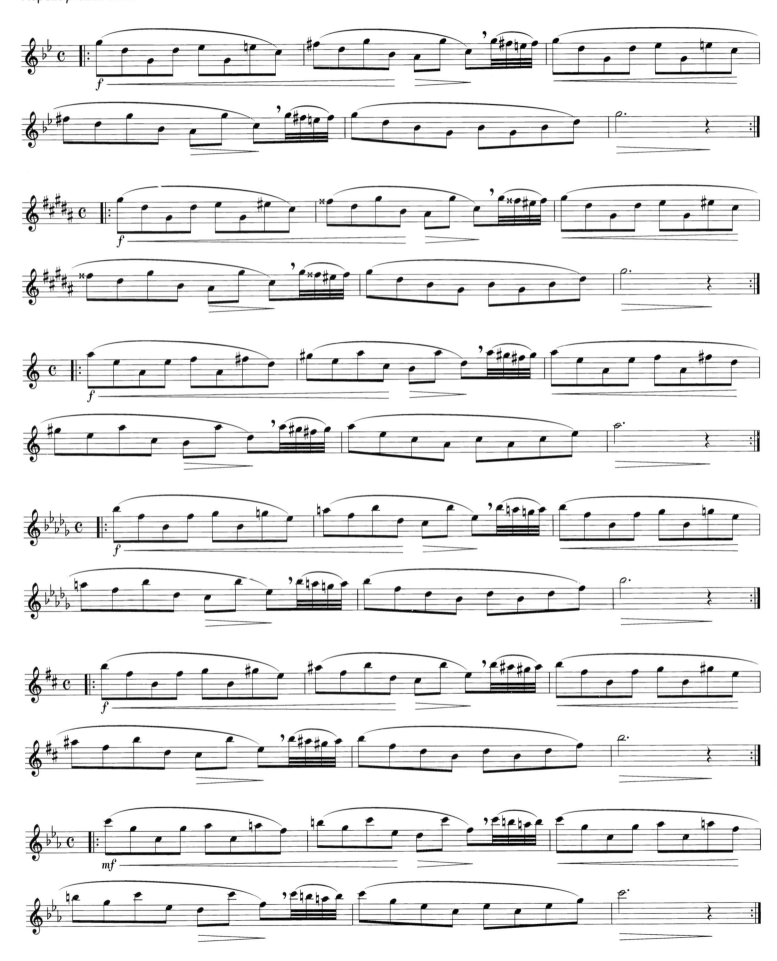

SECTION 2
Scales And Scale Exercises

Why do we spend time on scales?
There are many reasons, but the one that hit me hardest was when some years ago, I spent a week at the British Museum Reading Room, for the purpose of listing all the music for one or two flutes and continuo written before the year 1800. I started on Monday afternoon and by Friday morning I had only reached the letter D or E and had already collected a huge list of sonatas and suites. Later, looking through the European Library Lists, I tried to calculate how many pieces *world-wide* may have been written for this combination. It might be more than 80,000, and *all* were written using common scales and arpeggios.

It follows that if we practise scales and arpeggios regularly, we are simultaneously learning a huge number of pieces. Scales and arpeggios *must* be a good investment!

> The cue size notes in each scale can be omitted if preferred.

1 Major Scales to top B or D

Omit the small bracketed notes throughout if you are unfamiliar with top D.

C major

* Practise playing top E without the D♯ key – it's flatter.
** When slurring from top B to C, use the B fingering but remove the thumb.

D♭ major

D major

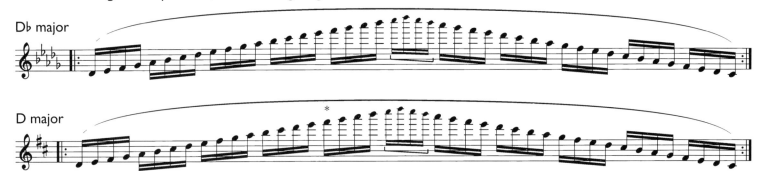

* Use the 3rd finger for F♯ in the 3rd octave only – this is also flatter.

E♭ major

E major

F major

F♯ major

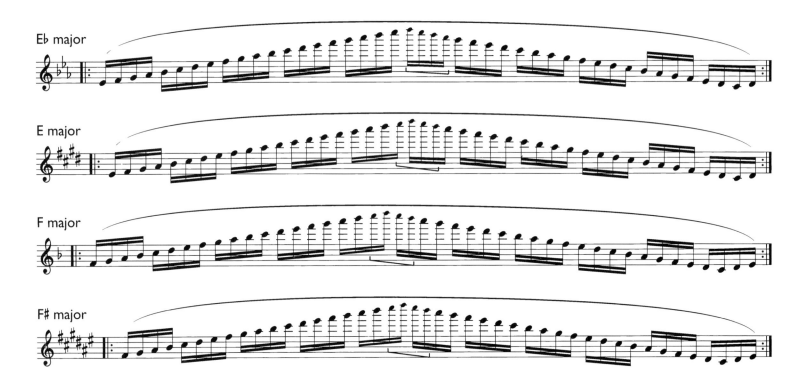

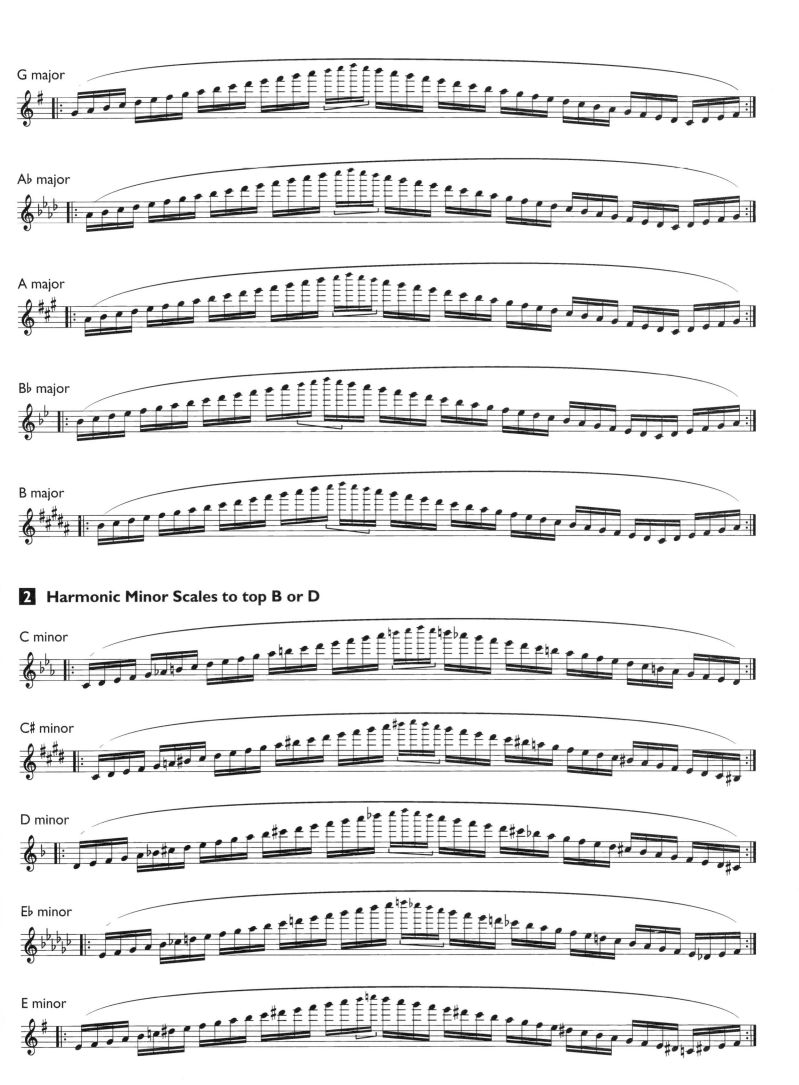

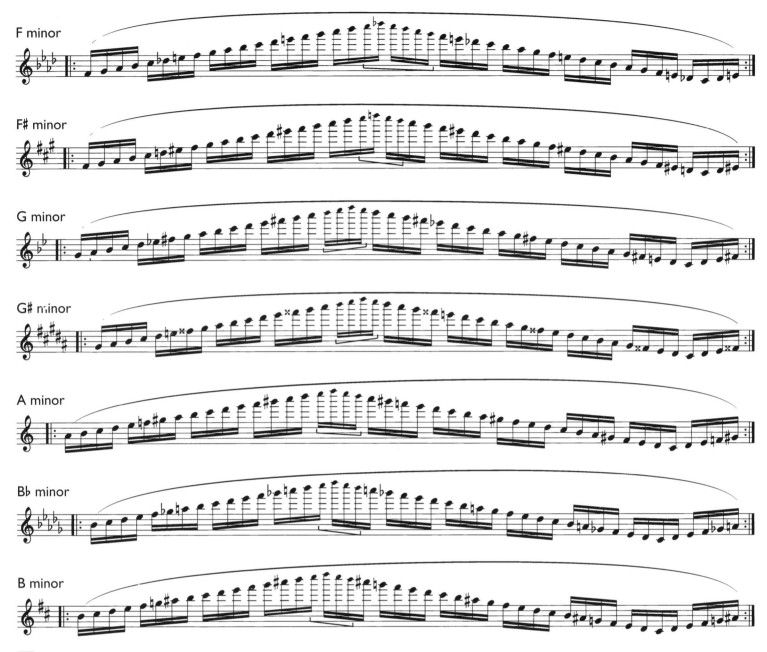

3 Whole Tone Scales

These are used by many composers and most frequently in 20th century French orchestral repertoire.

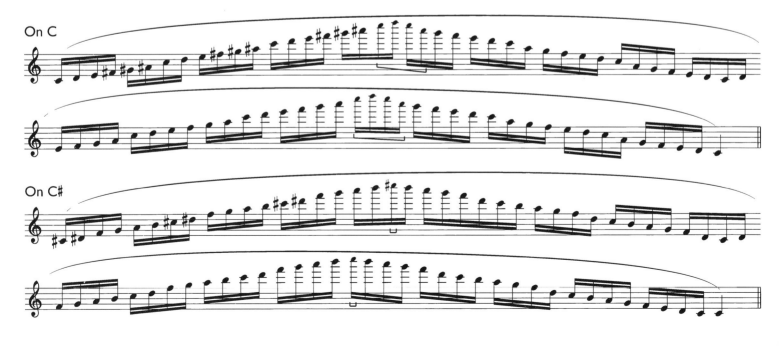

4 **Major Scales to top B or D in thirds**

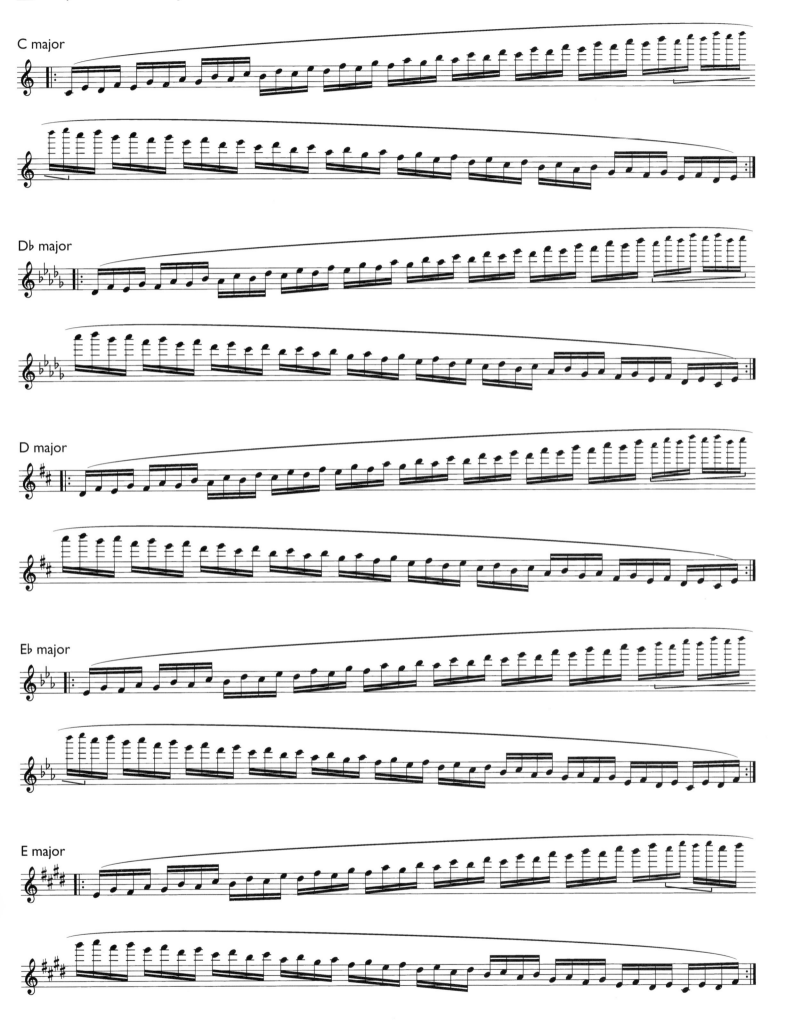

15

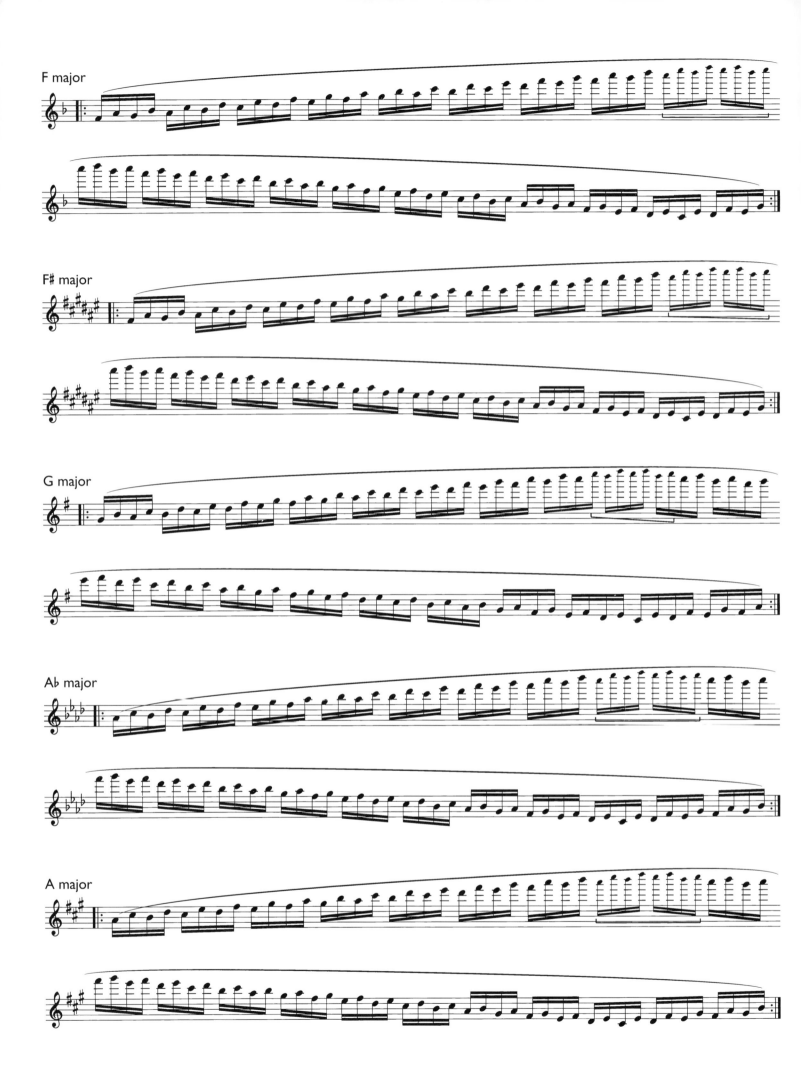

Bb major

B major

5 Minor Scales to top B or D in thirds

C minor

C# minor

D minor

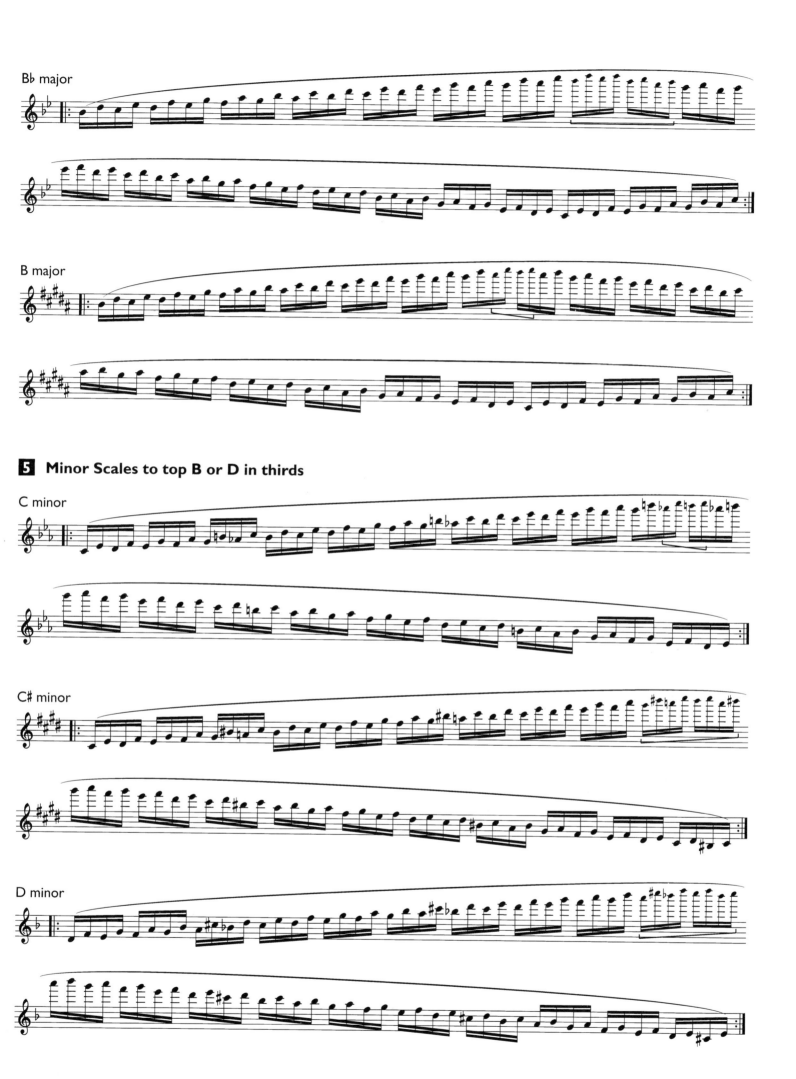

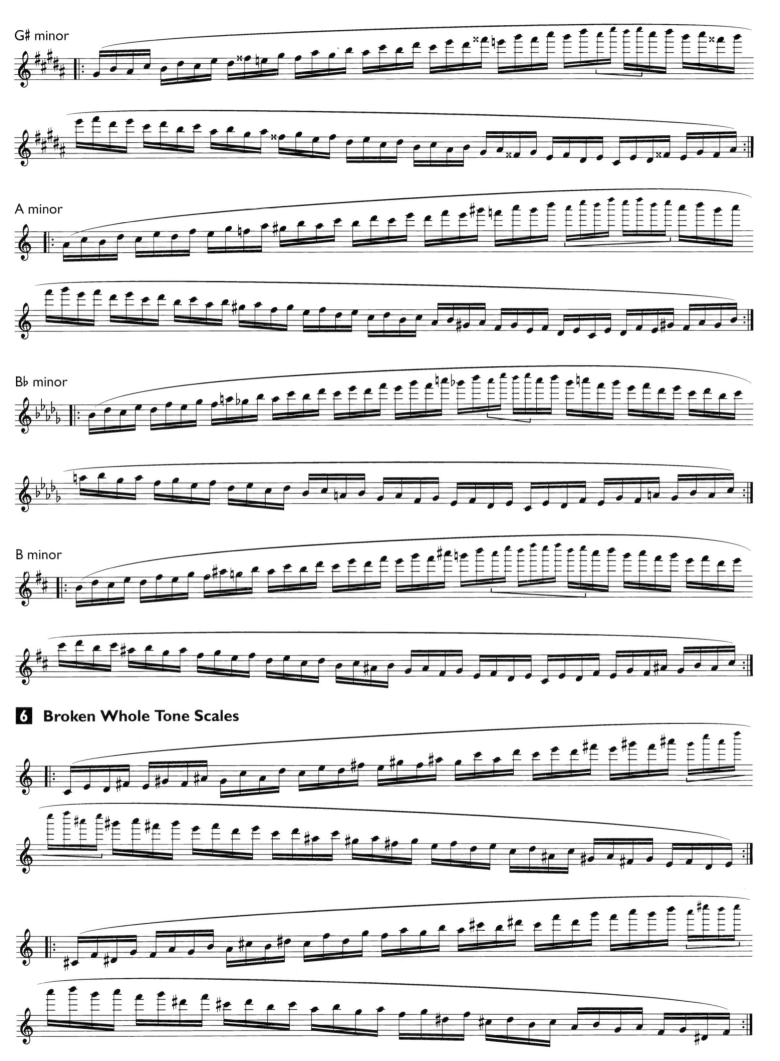

Daily exercises on scales

7 Major Scale Exercise

Refer to the Practice Card for articulation suggestions.
Practise also in these forms:

* Take care to use the D♯ key for E. It is also a way to balance the flute when moving between octaves.

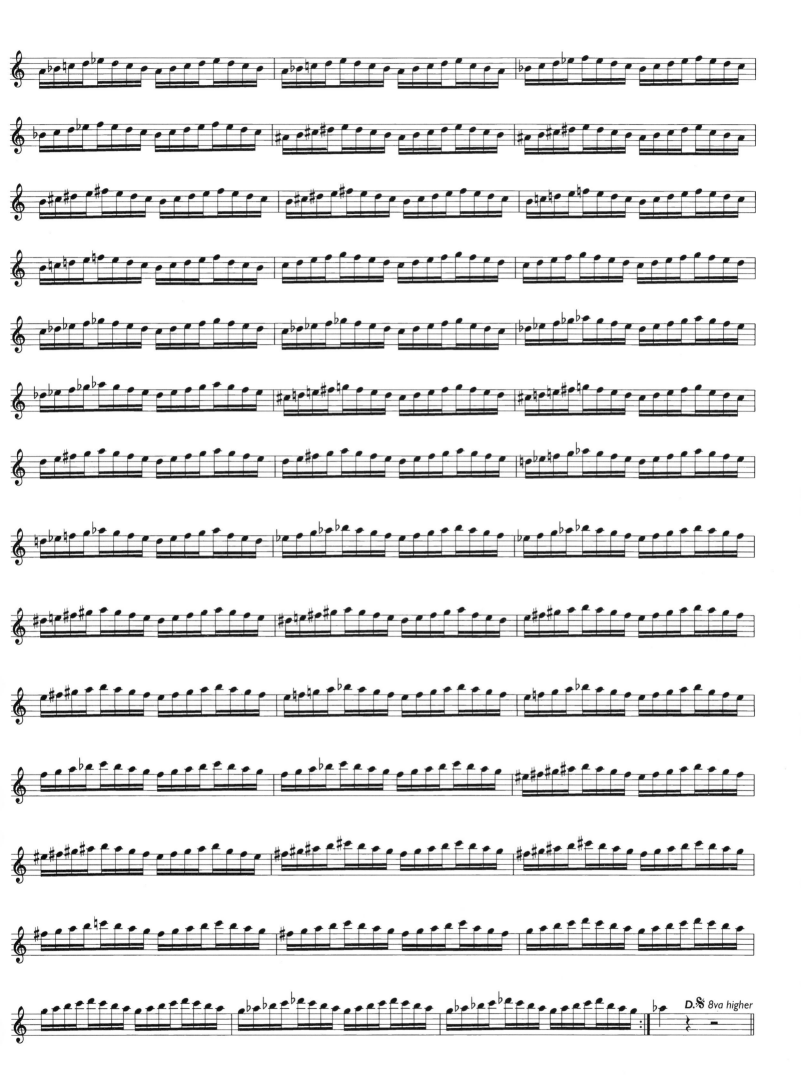

8 Minor Scale Exercise

Refer to the Practice Card for articulation suggestions.

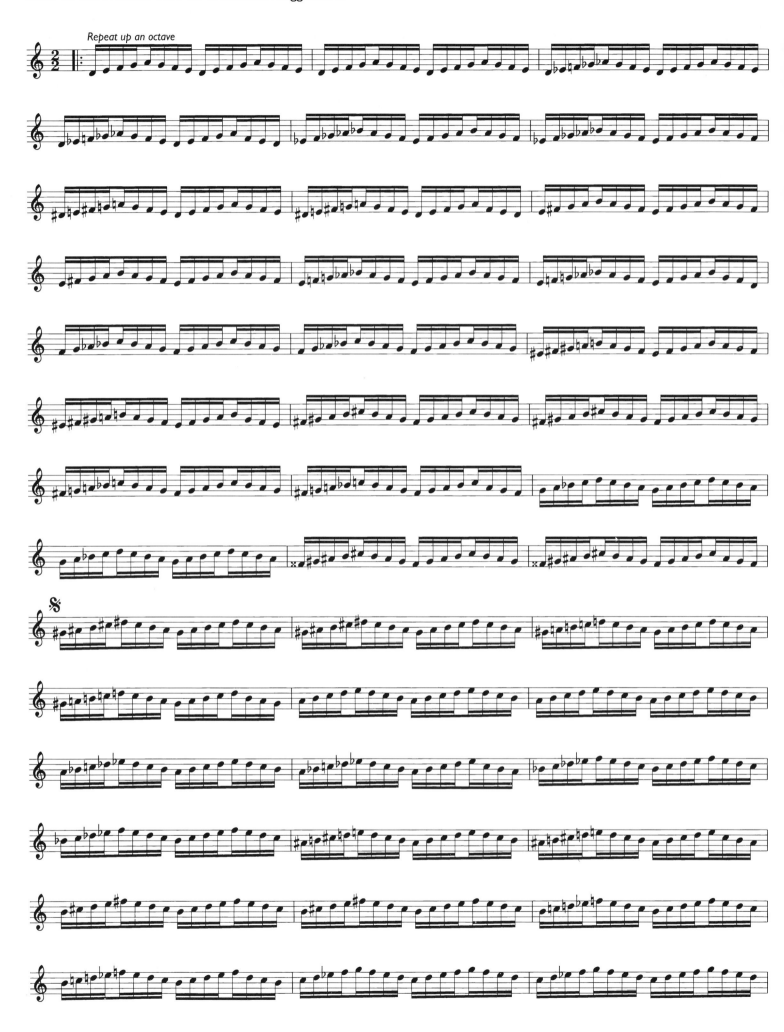

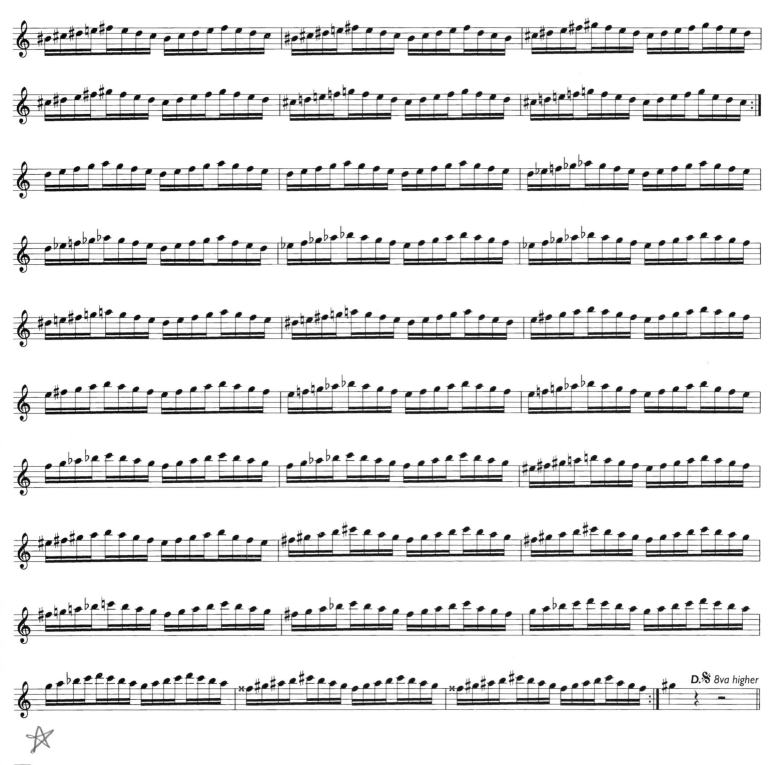

9 Major and Minor Scale Exercises

Refer to the Practice Card for articulation suggestions.

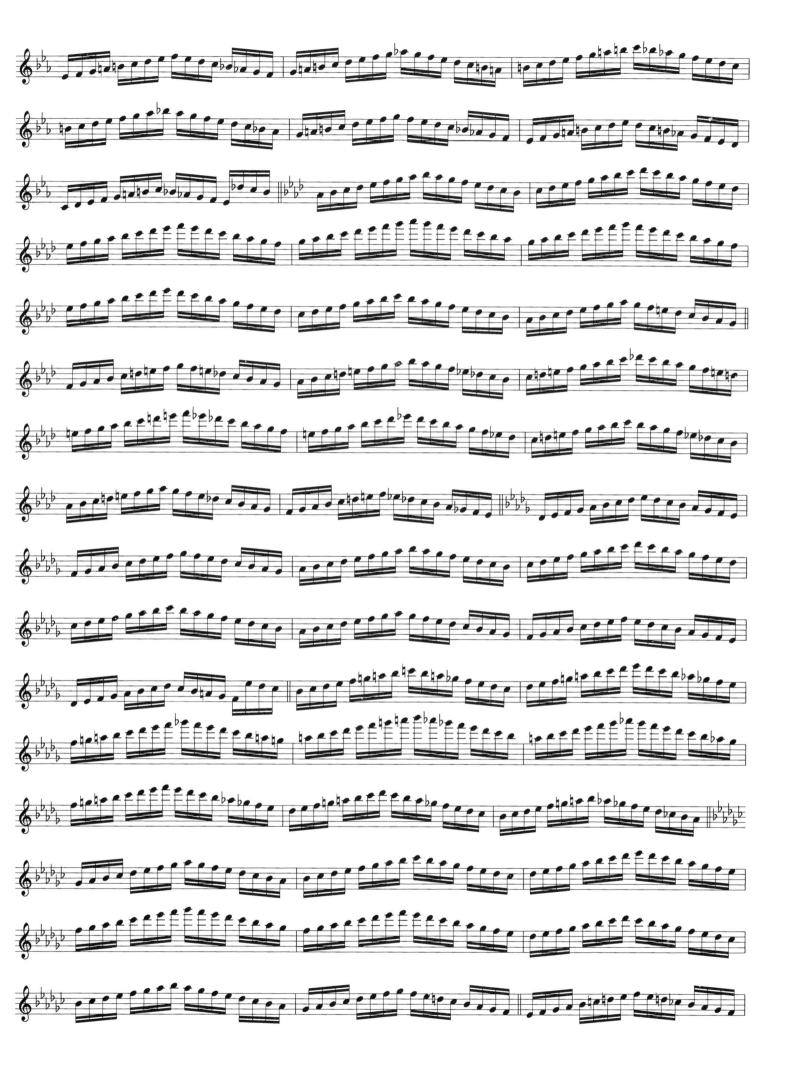

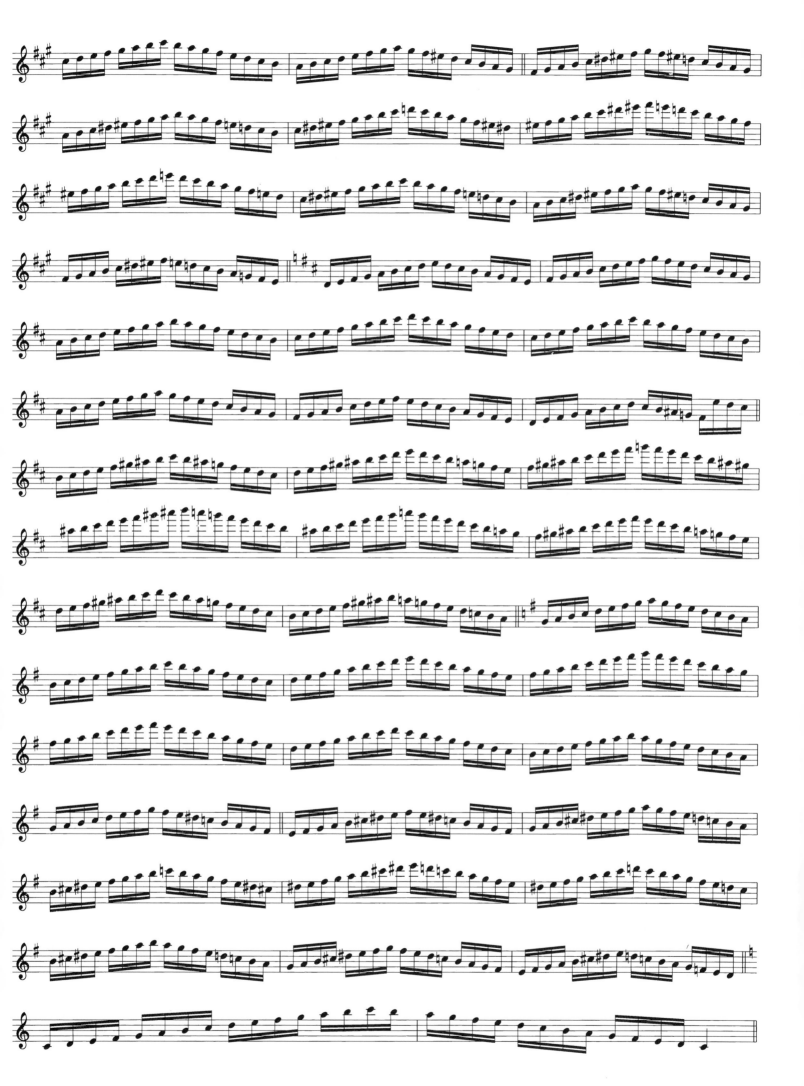

10 No.1 from Seven Daily Exercises (Reichert)

Practise using these articulations:

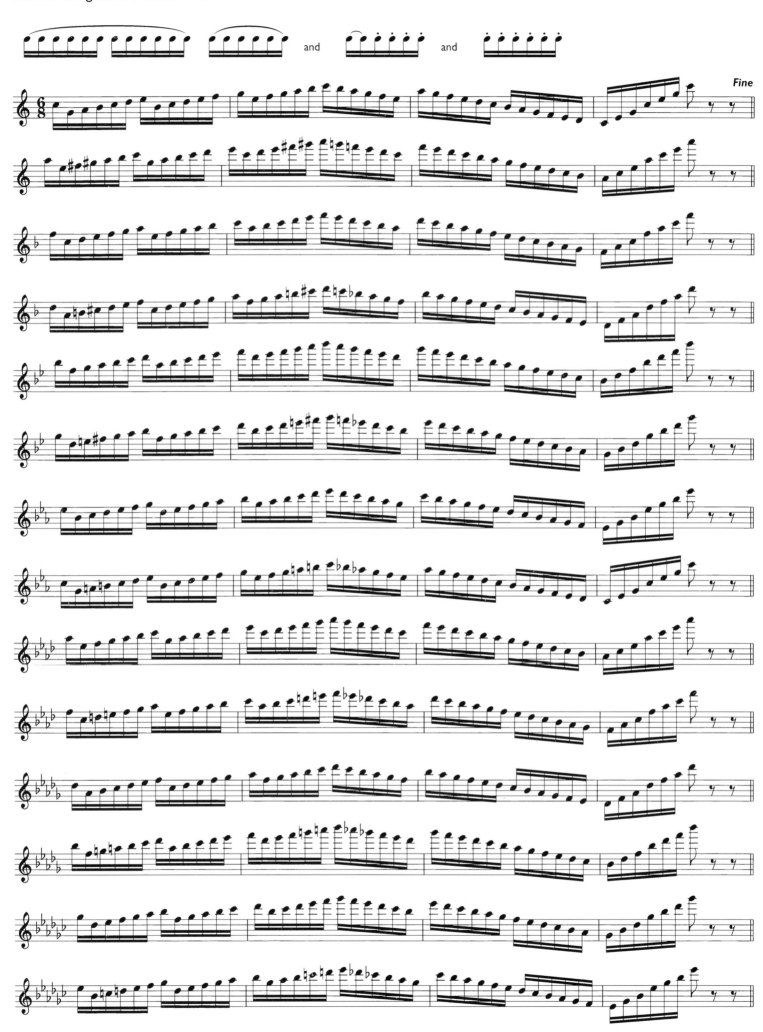

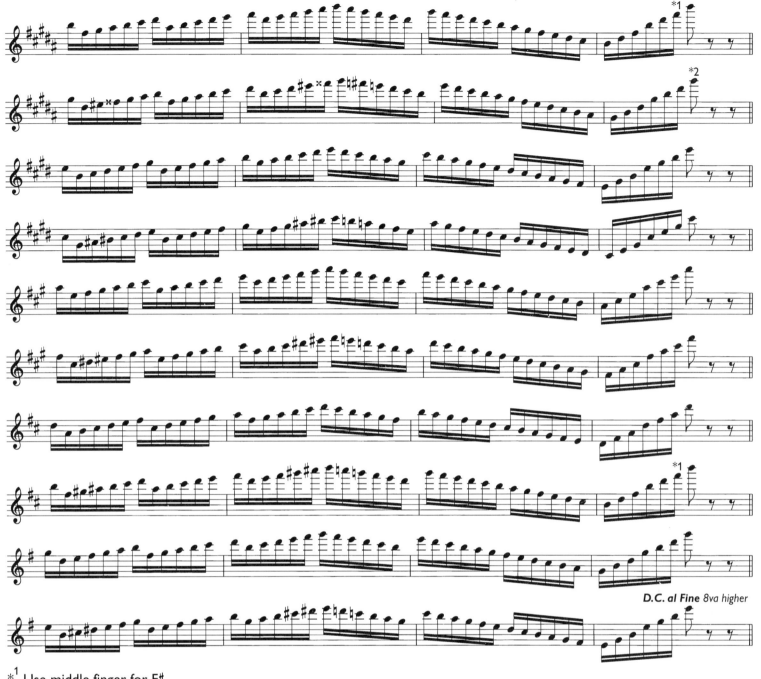

*¹ Use middle finger for F♯.

*² Use 'long' A♭:

11 Cascading Major and Minor Scales

Refer to the Practice Card for changes of articulation.
Vary your routine by starting at D♭ then making a Da Capo.

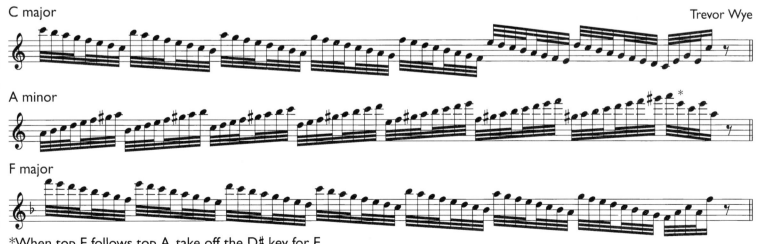

*When top E follows top A, take off the D♯ key for E.

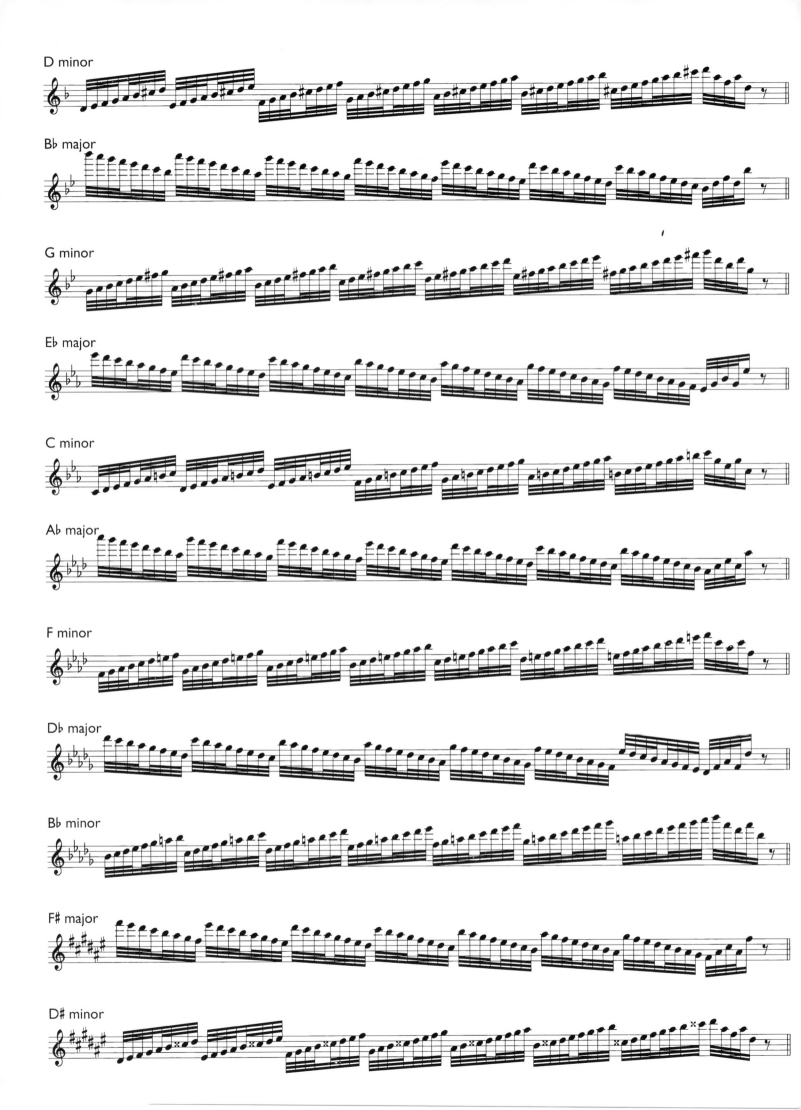

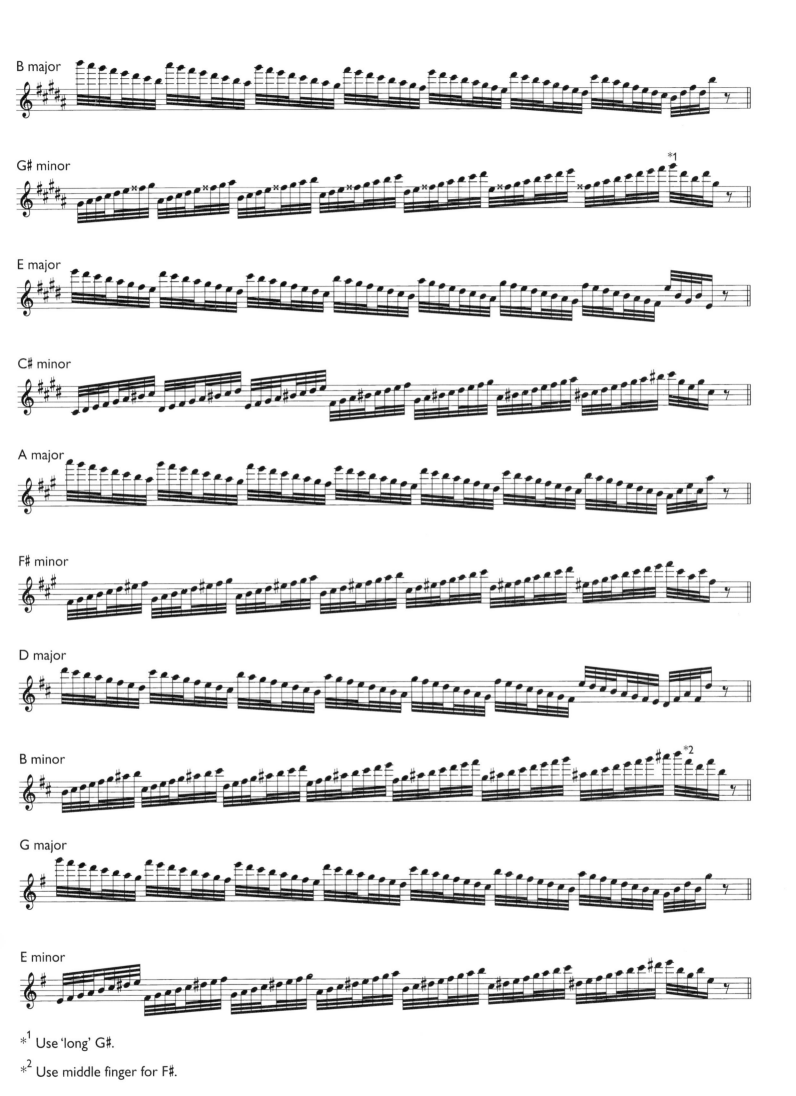

*1 Use 'long' G#.

*2 Use middle finger for F#.

SECTION 3
Arpeggios

1 Arpeggios to top B and low C
Refer to the Practice Card for variations of articulation.
When practising these arpeggios, it is useful to include the various alternative fingerings
for ease and fluidity, and also because they are in tune! Examples are given throughout.
In general, D major is more in tune using the middle finger, flatter fingering for F♯.

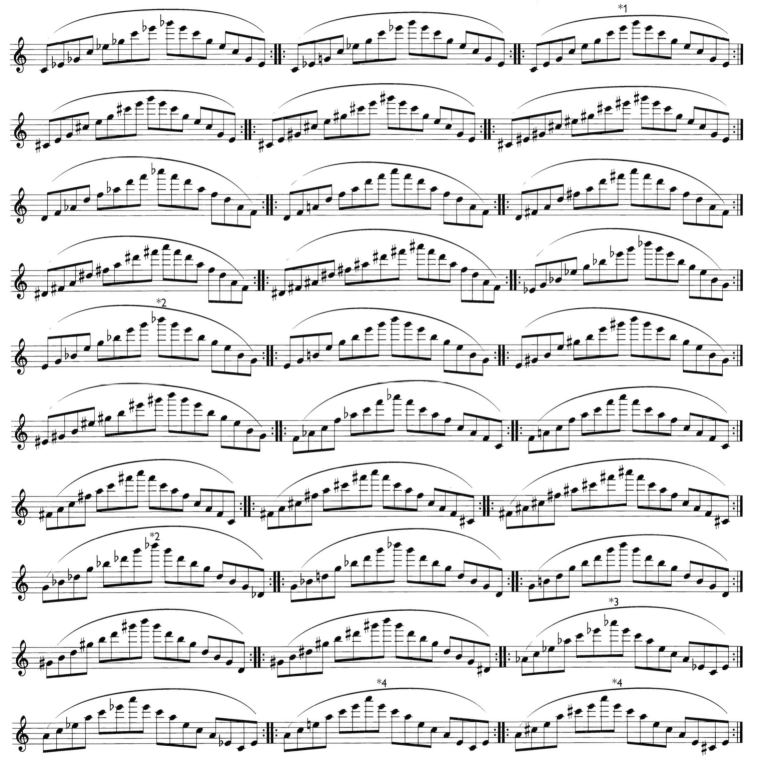

*¹ Top E is more in tune (less sharp) without the D♯ key.

*² To gain familiarity with a useful fingering, practise the so-called 'Mignon fingering' for top B♭ when playing *pp*. It is sharp and will require flattening:

*³ Use the 'long' A♭ here:

*⁴ Play E without the D♯ key to facilitate the leap.

*5 Practise 'leaning' on the trill key for B♭ to gain speed.

*6 Use middle finger F# here to smooth the interval.

2 Extended Arpeggios to top D and low B

Refer to the Practice Card for articulation suggestions.

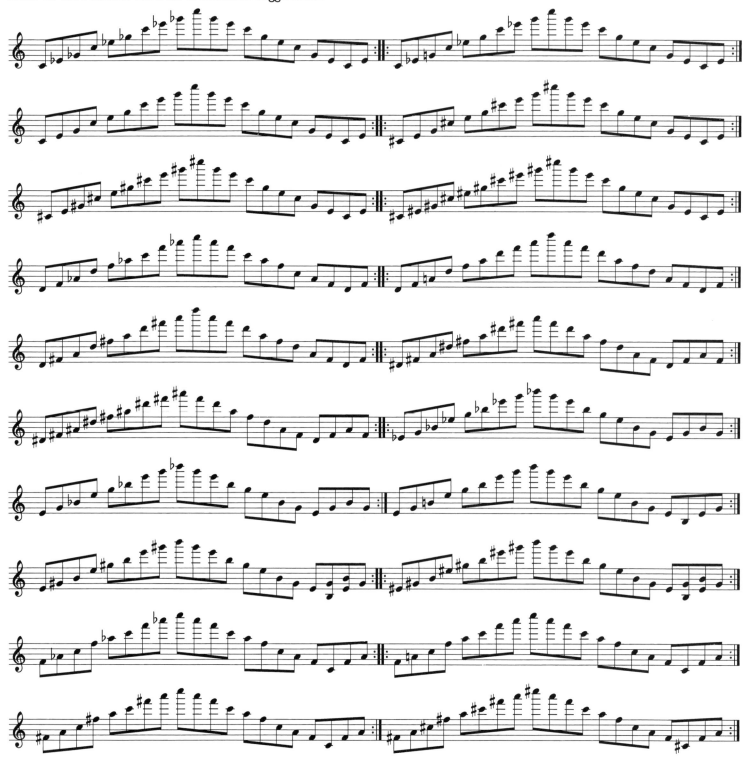

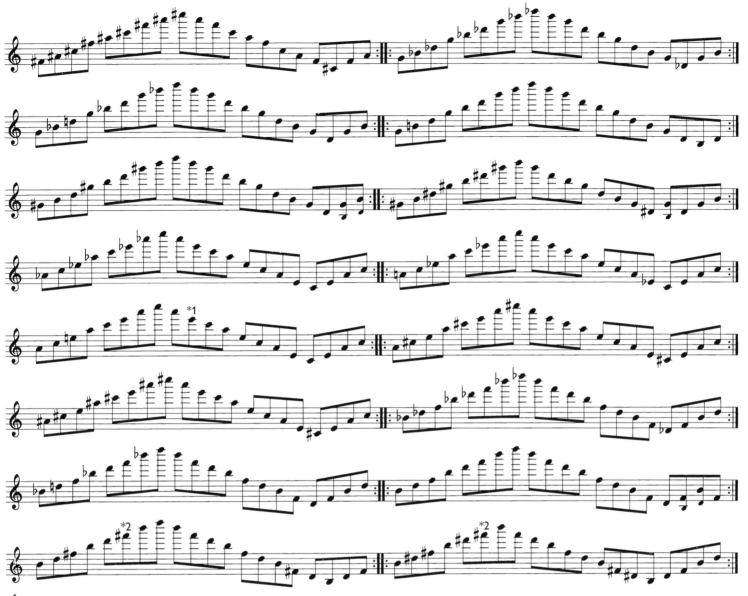

*¹ Play E without the D♯ key to facilitate the leap.

*² Middle finger F♯.

3 Augmented 5th Arpeggios

Refer to the Practice Card for articulation suggestions.

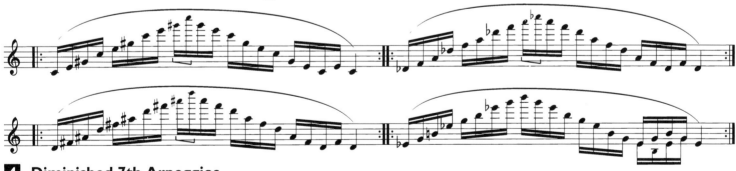

4 Diminished 7th Arpeggios

5 Arpeggios of the 7th

The first bar is the 'form' of the exercise. Practise it with all the different accidentals.

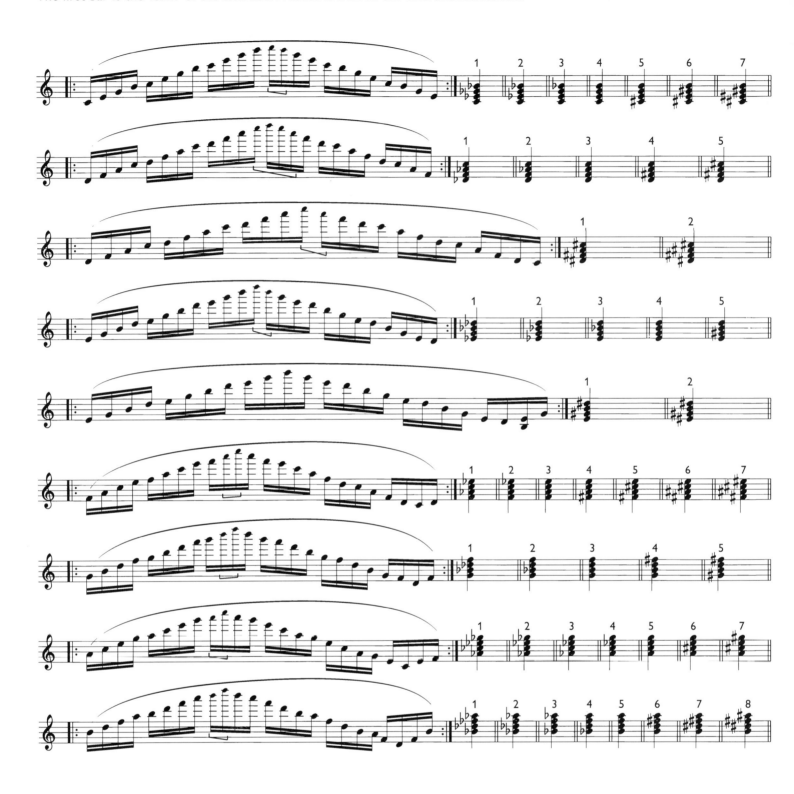

6 Arpeggio Study 1

Refer to the Practice Card for articulation suggestions.

a)

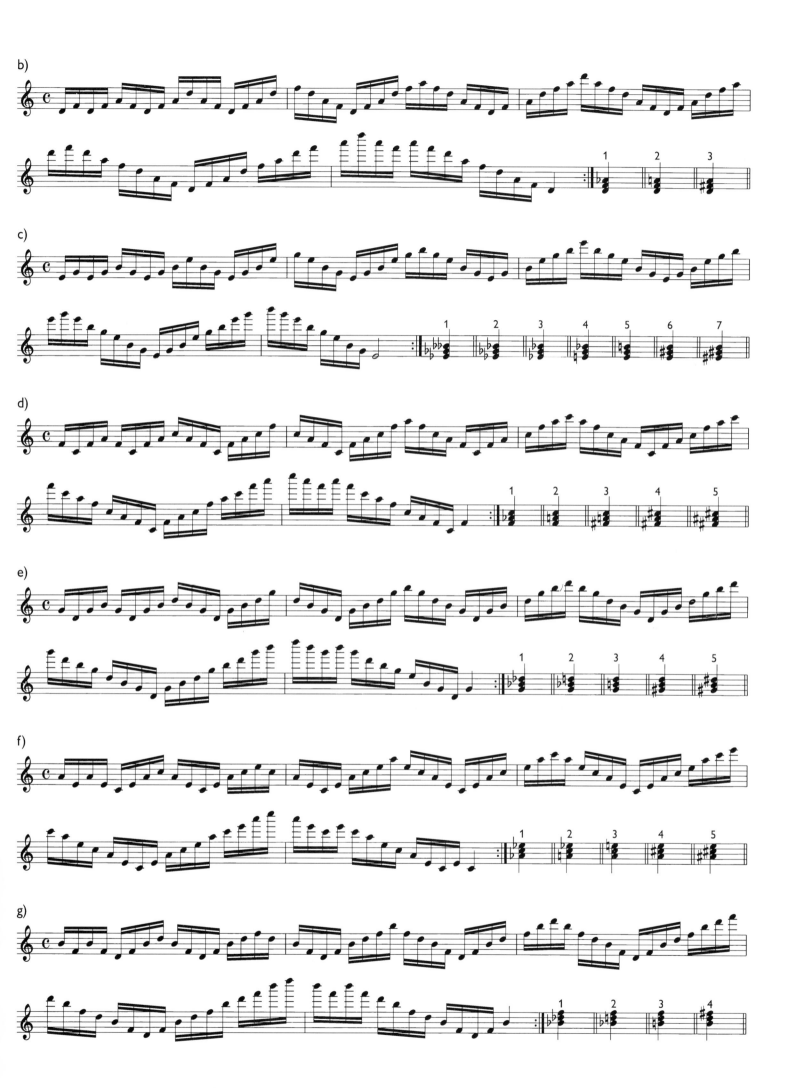

7 Arpeggio Study 2
Refer to the Practice Card for articulation suggestions.

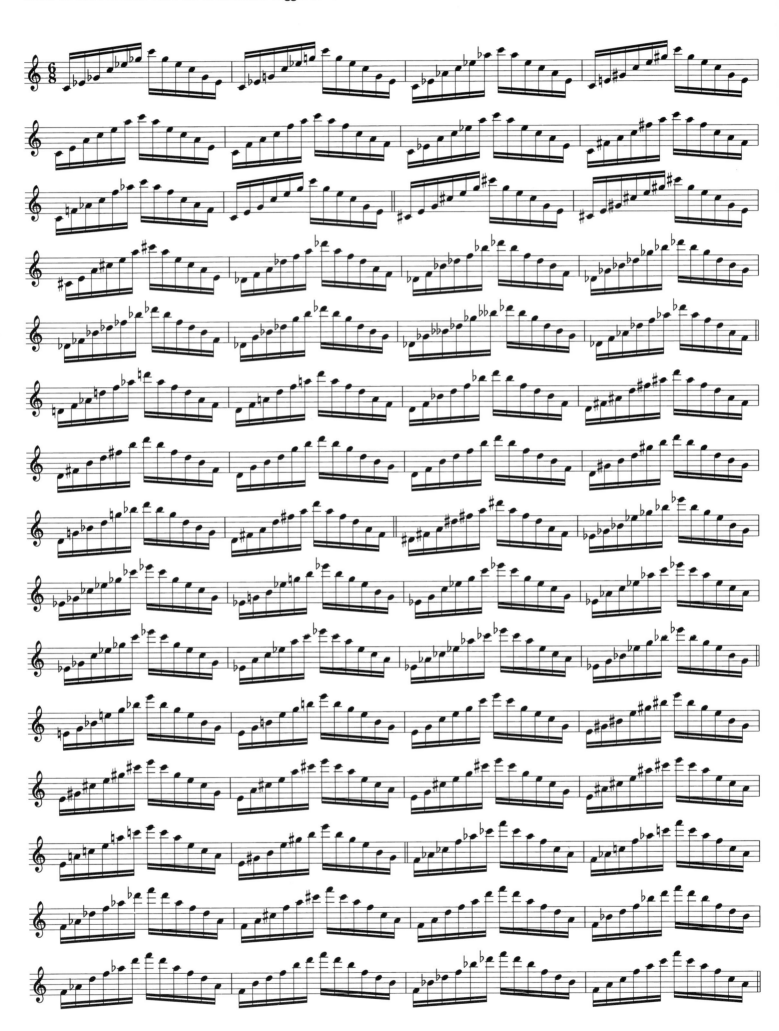

38

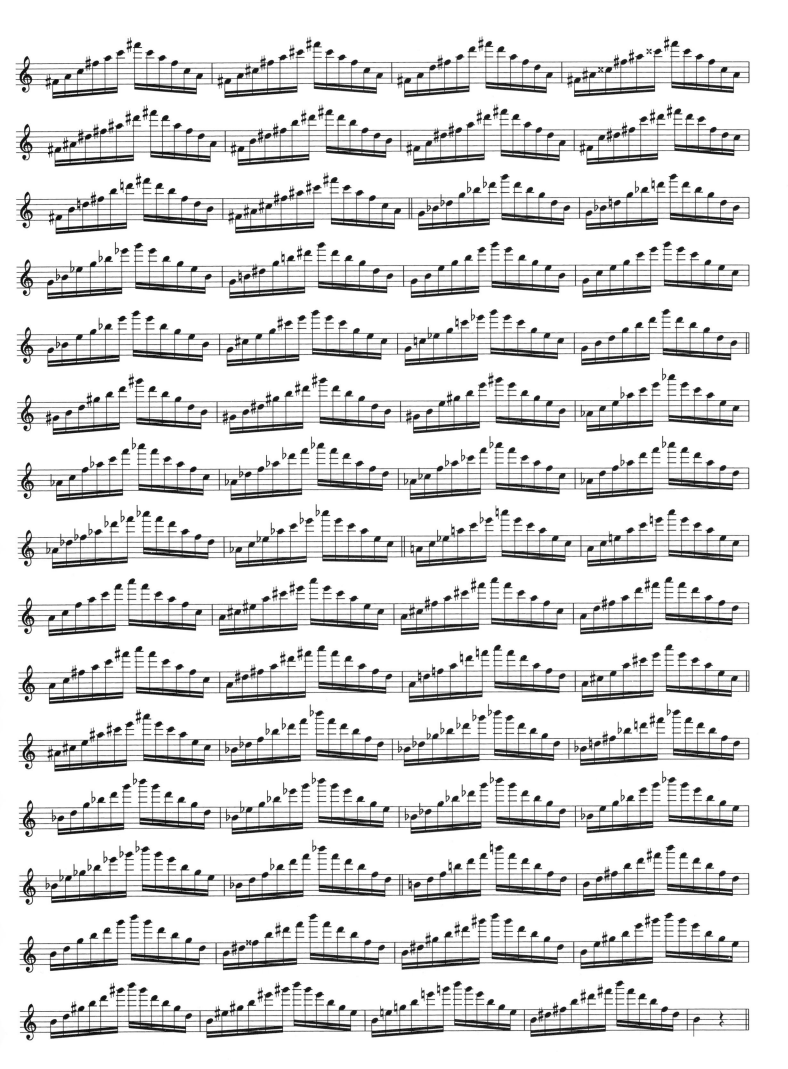

8 **Daily Exercise No.1 (Maquarre)**
Refer to the Practice Card for articulation suggestions.

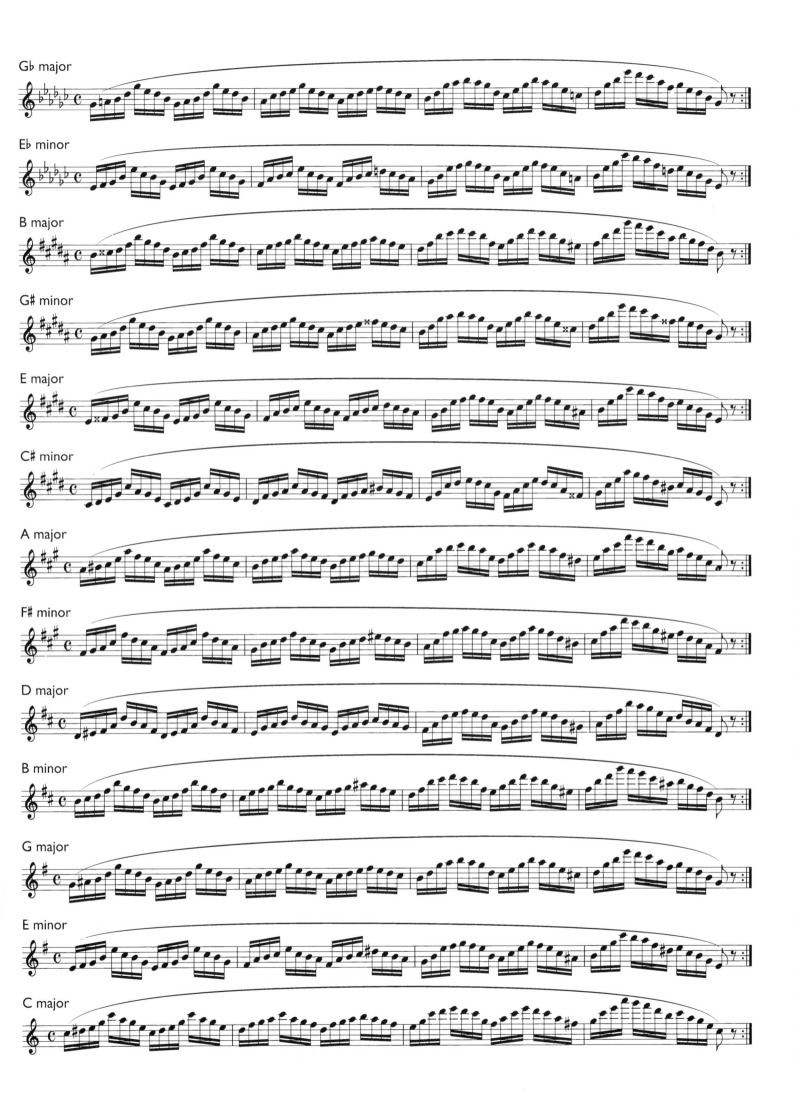

9 **Daily Exercise No.5 (Maquarre)**
Refer to the Practice Card for articulation suggestions.

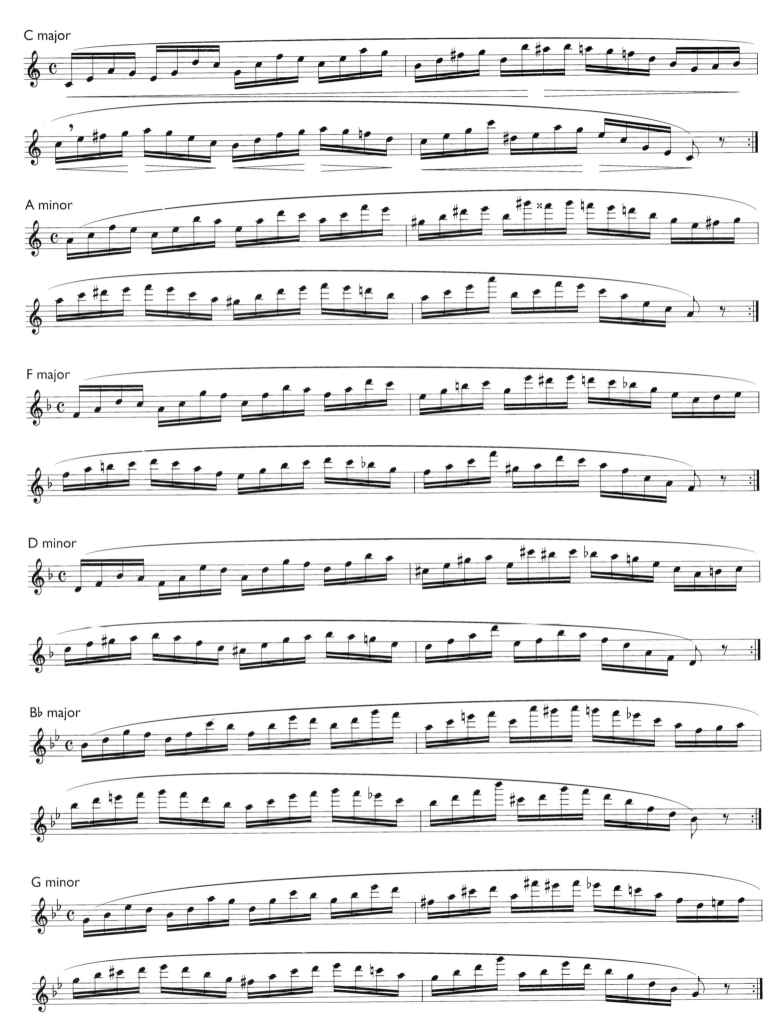

42

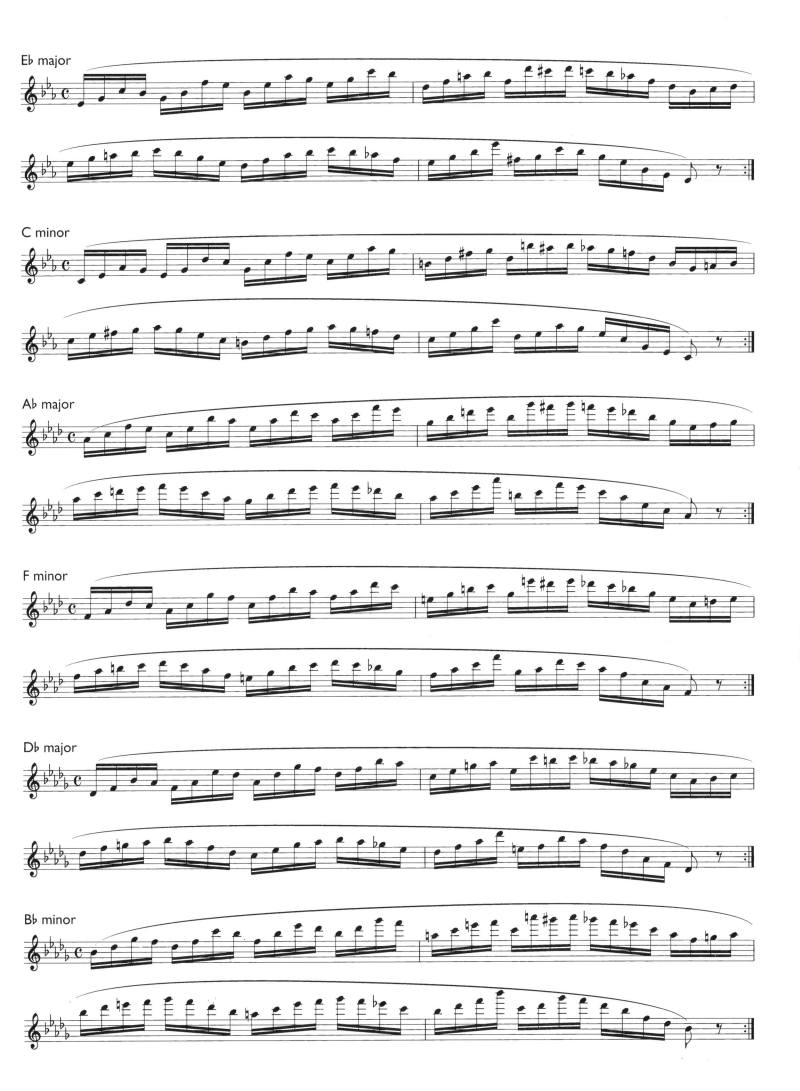

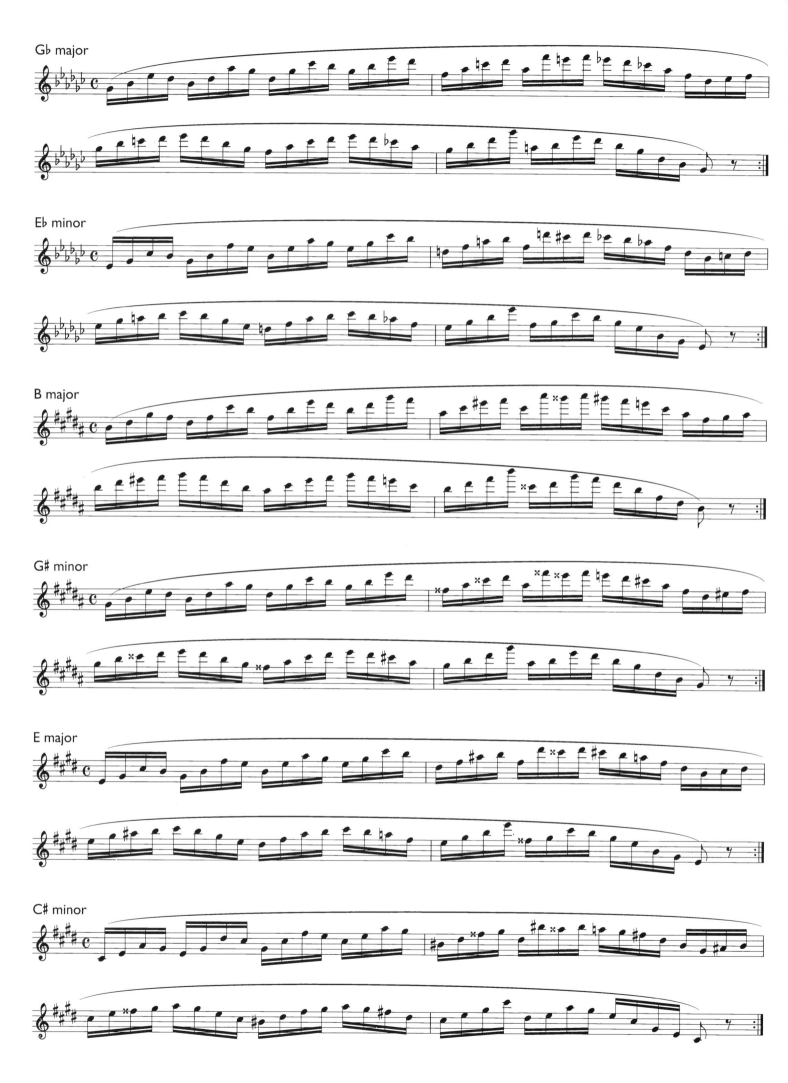

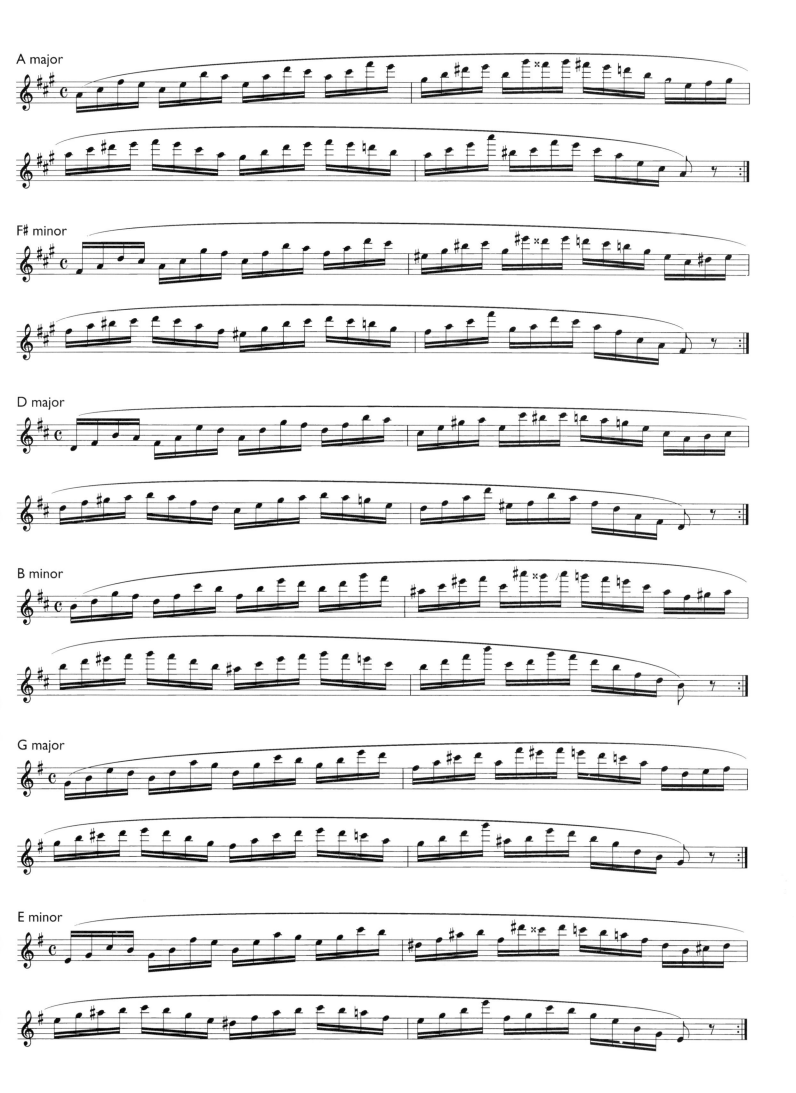

10 Broken Arpeggios

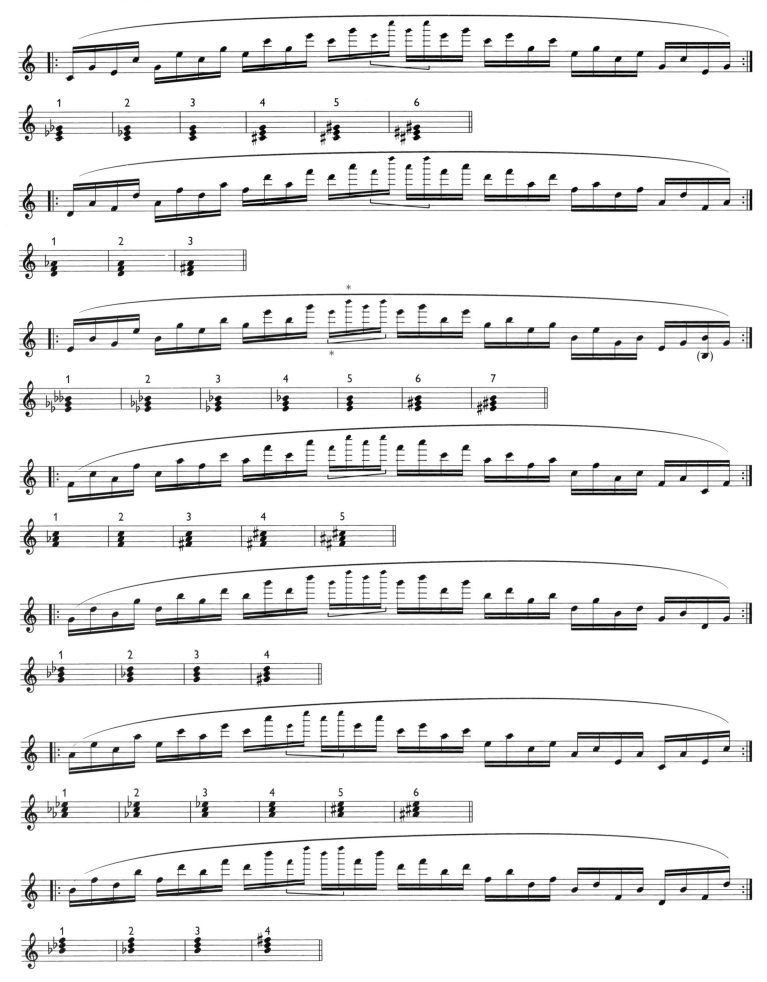

* When moving from top E♭ to B♭ it is better to become familiar with a useful forte B♭.
First play top E♭, then remove the 2nd finger of the left hand, and at the same time, 'lean' on the first trill key without taking your finger off the 'F' key, and take your finger off the G♯ key.

11 Broken 7th Arpeggios

See note on previous page about top B♭. Also use the middle finger
F♯ when moving to top B, and the long A♭ fingering after E♭.
Top E is better in tune (flatter) without the D♯ key.

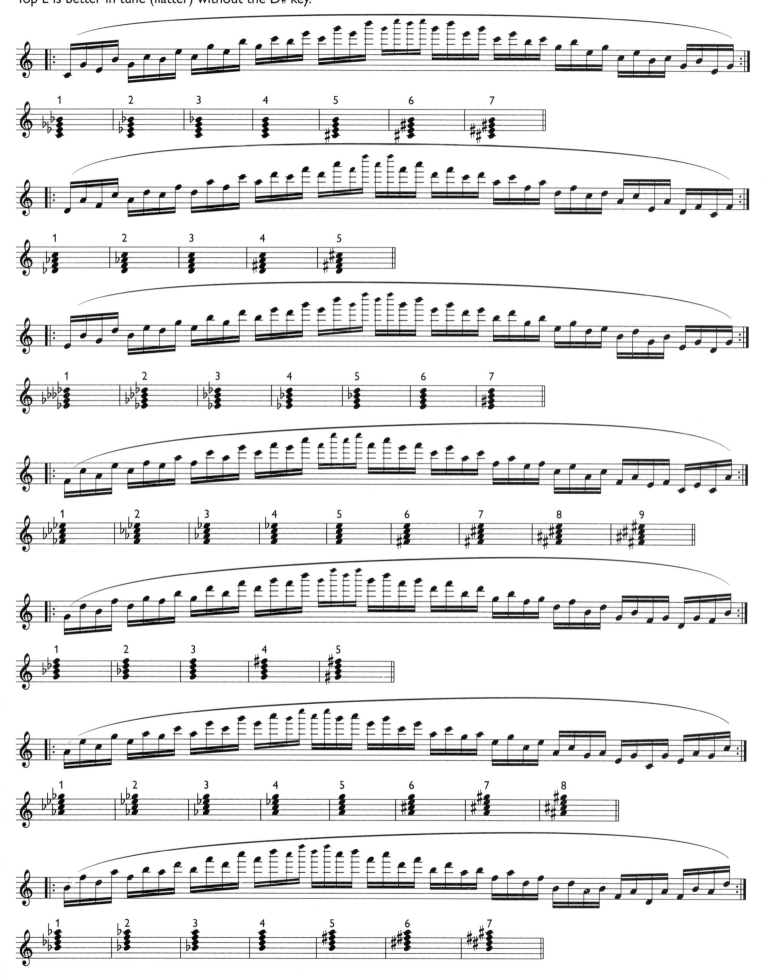

47

12 Broken Augmented 5th Arpeggios

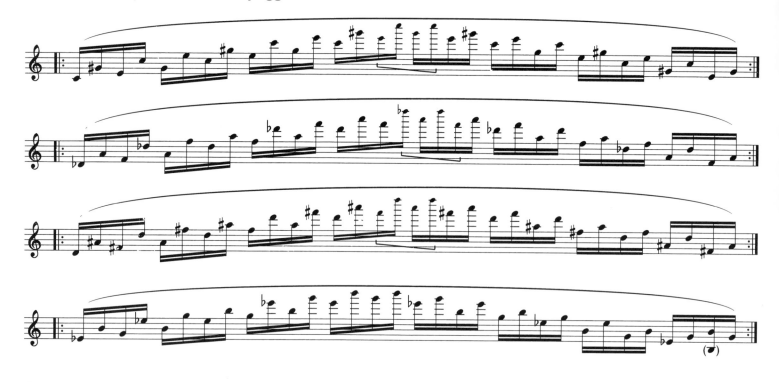

13 Broken Diminished 7th Arpeggios

14 Broken Arpeggio Study
Refer to the Practice Card for articulation suggestions.

15 **No.2 from Seven Daily Exercises (Reichert)**

This Reichert study is a fine tone exercise when played slowly.
It was a favourite of Marcel Moyse (see page 5 in the TONE section).
It can be practised in these two ways as well:

It can be used for *pianissimo* practice in the 2nd and 3rd octaves:

Refer to the Practice Card for articulation suggestions.

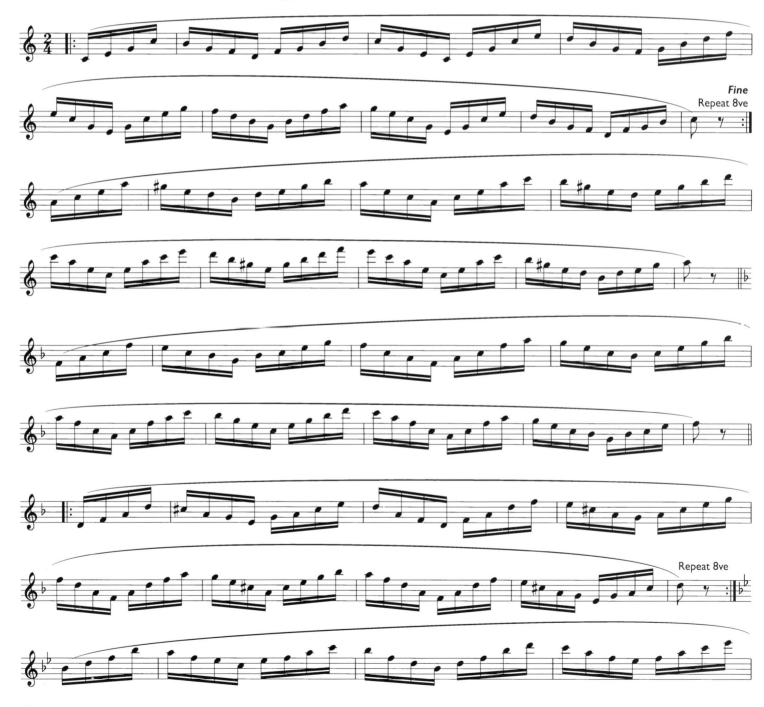

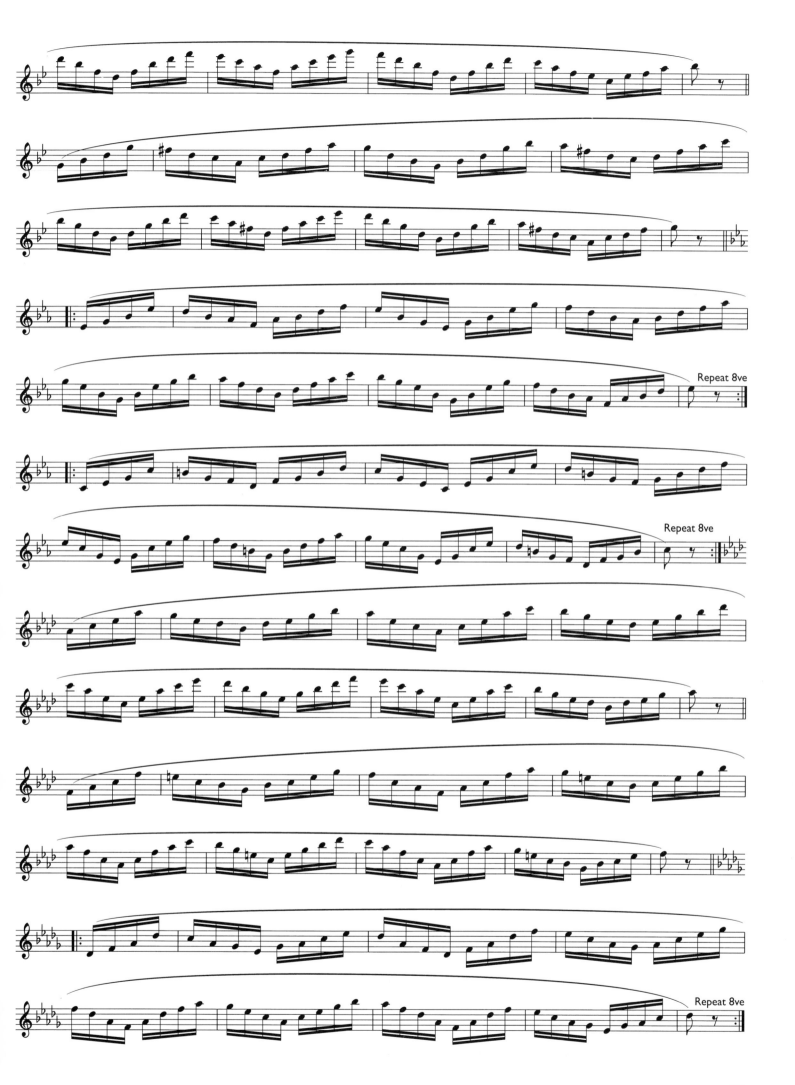

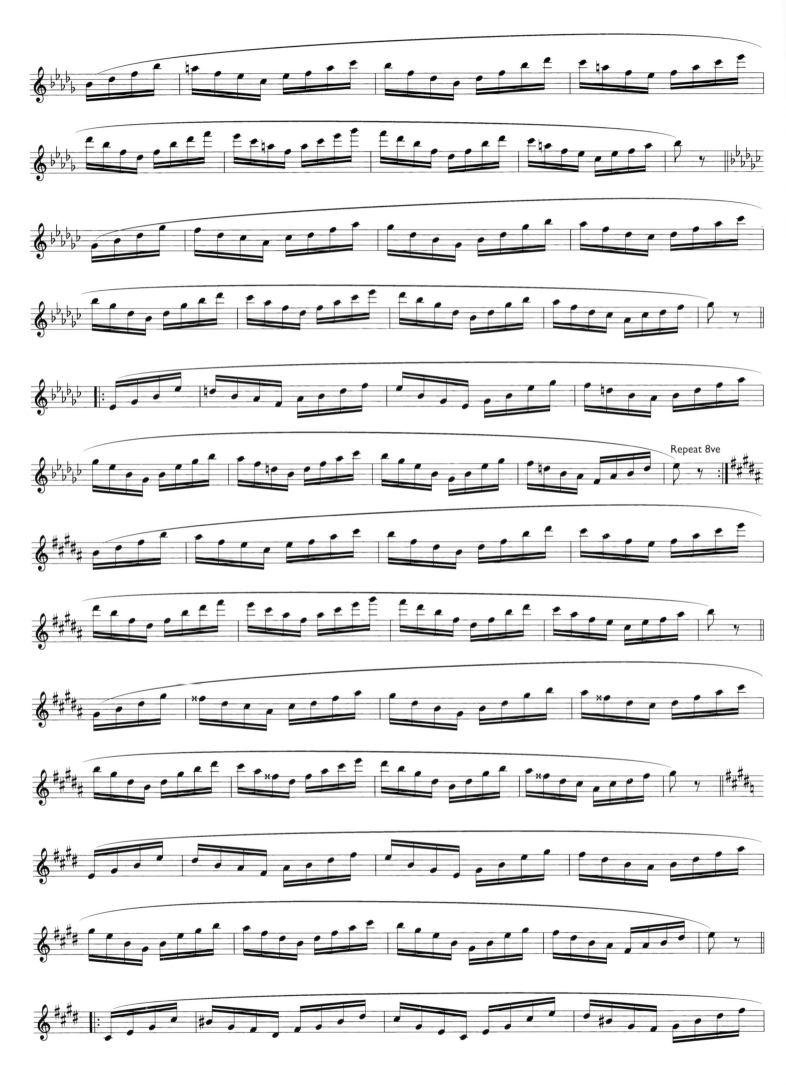

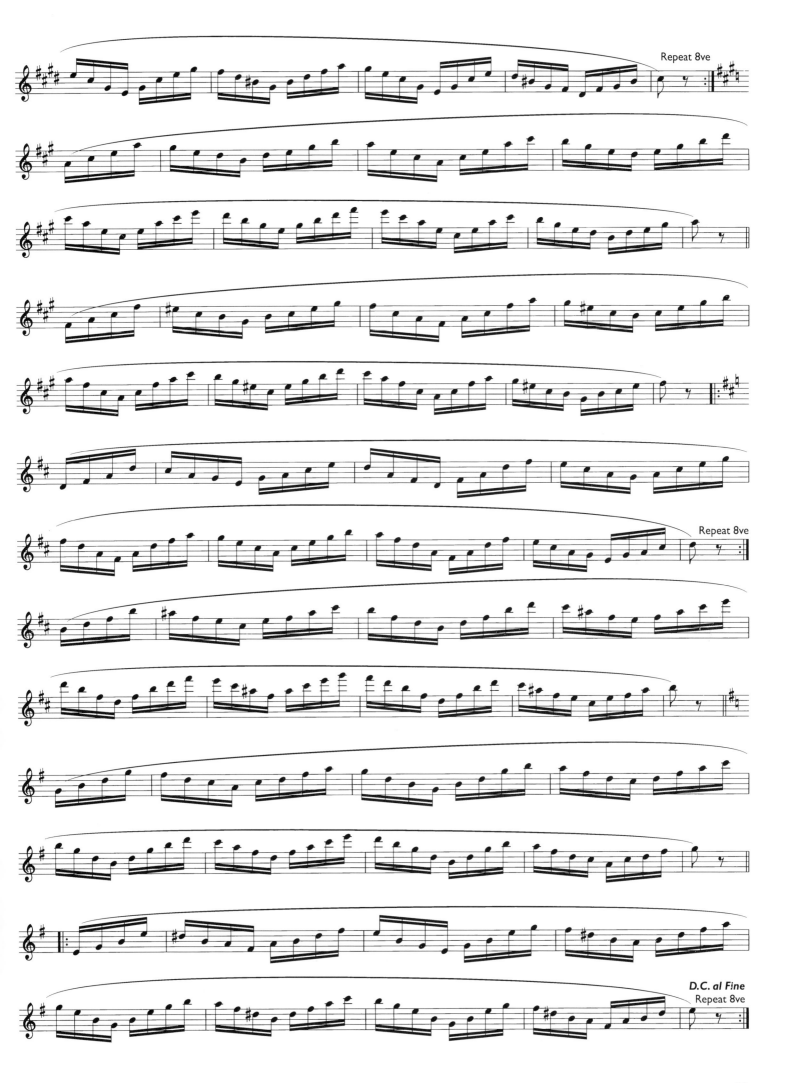

16 No.4 from Seven Daily Exercises (Reichert)

This is another which is both fascinating and beneficial to use as an expressive tone exercise or warm-up. It can also be played like this:

Refer to the Practice Card for articulation suggestions.

17 No.5 from Seven Daily Exercises (Reichert)

This too, can be altered rhythmically and turned into a fine study for expression, intonation or triple tonguing, as well as flexibility.
Here are some suggestions:

Refer to the Practice Card for articulation suggestions.

18 No.7 from Seven Daily Exercises (Reichert)
This exercise may also be practised with single tonguing throughout.

19 No.1 from Twelve Studies (Boehm)

This study can be practised *legato*, and with single and triple tonguing.

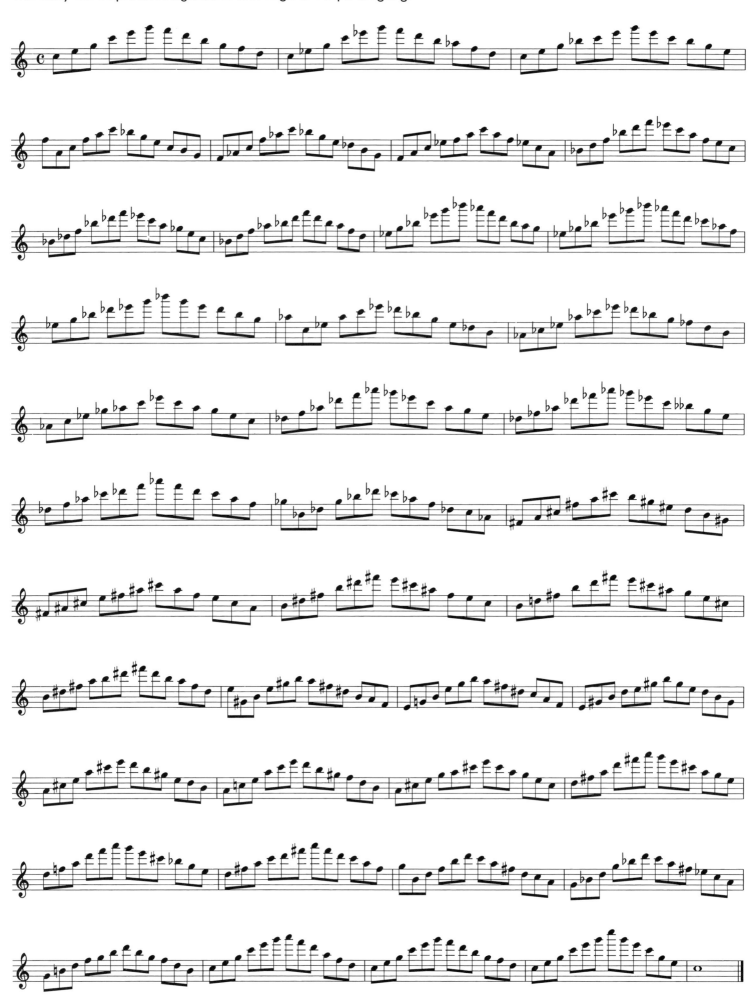

20 No.11 from Twelve Studies (Boehm)

This may be practised in the following five ways:

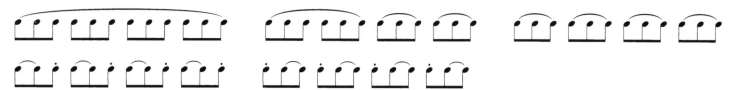

This study can also be varied by making the second bar of each line a minor arpeggio.

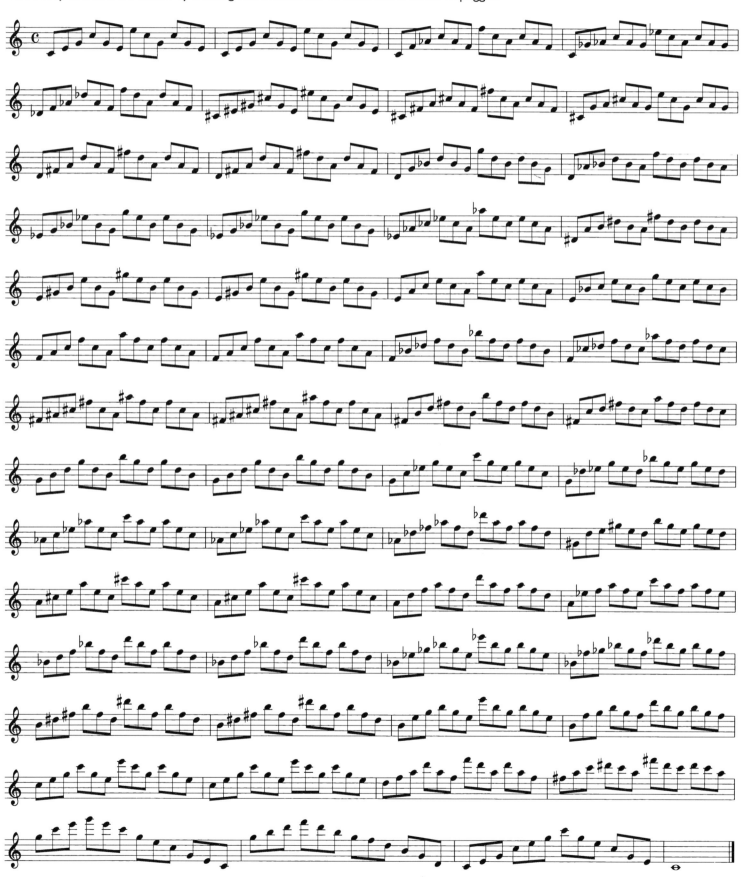

SECTION 4
Chromatic Exercises

1 Chromatic Scale to top C or D
Refer to the Practice Card for articulation suggestions.

2 Broken Chromatic Scales

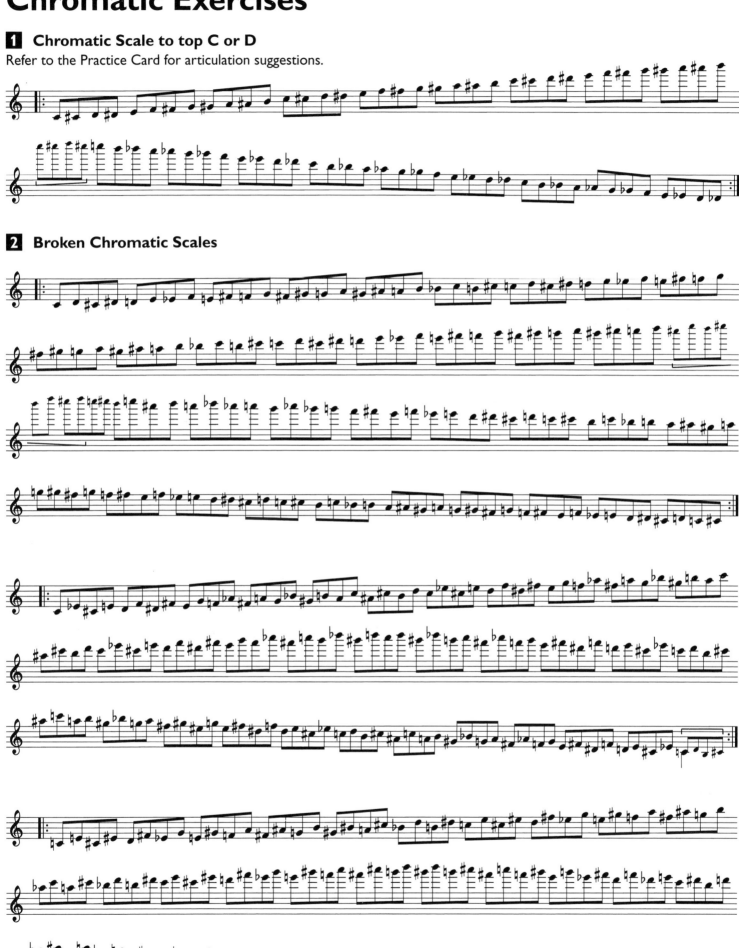

3 No.6 from Seven Daily Exercises (Reichert)

Refer to the Practice Card for articulation suggestions.

4 Four Chromatic Sequences
Also practise with the following articulations:

Refer to the Practice Card for articulation suggestions.

* Omit bracketed notes if your compass is to top B.

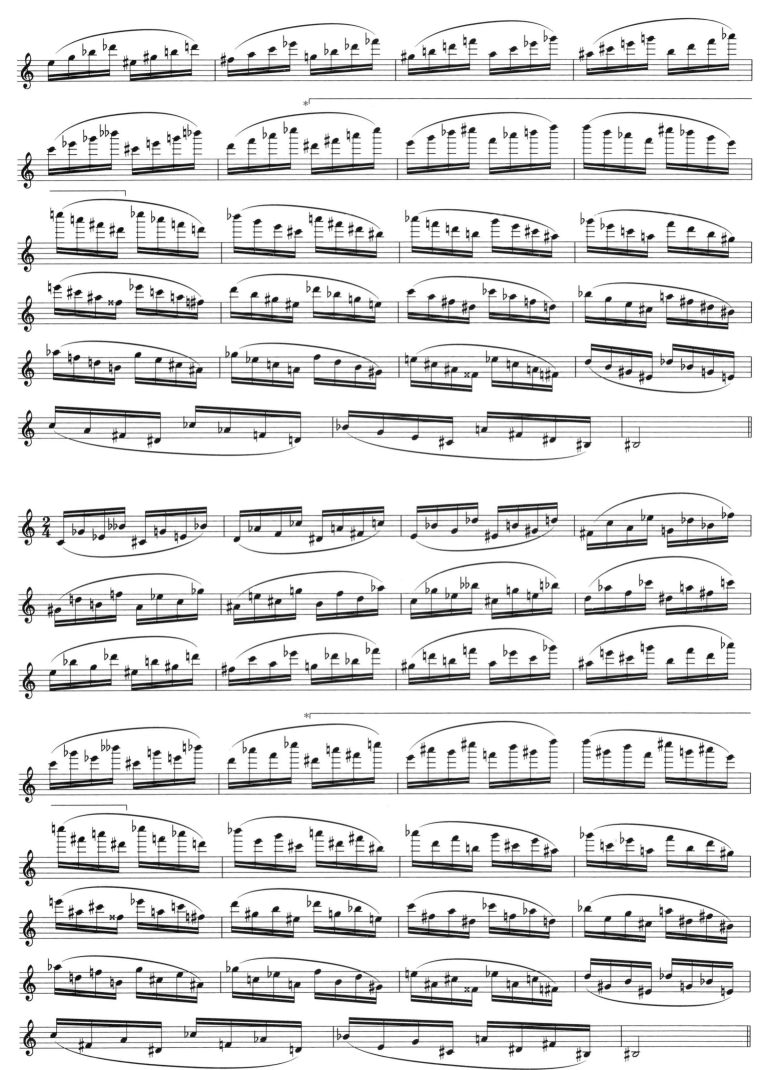

5 First Chromatic Study

To practise the 3rd octave, play 7–12 an octave higher,
and follow with 1–5 two octaves higher.
Refer to the Practice Card for articulation suggestions.

Trevor Wye

6 Second Chromatic Study

To practise the 3rd octave, repeat from No.12 in reverse order one octave higher (12, 11, 10, 9, 8, etc.).
Refer to the Practice Card for articulation suggestions.

Trevor Wye

SECTION 5

The Third Octave

Six Daily Exercises to top B, C or D after D.S. Wood:
Studies For Facilitating The Execution Of The Upper Notes On The Flute

Beginning with the first study, play through it to the highest point that
you reasonably can, and then try to add a higher note every week or so.
When Exercise 1 has been worked at for some time, it is better to *add*
the second study to it. This will lead to increased efficiency in the first exercise.

It is important to iron out any technical problems in the lower two octaves
before venturing into the third octave, and the practise of pages 20–23 is advised.

Refer to the Practice Card for articulation suggestions.

1 Scales

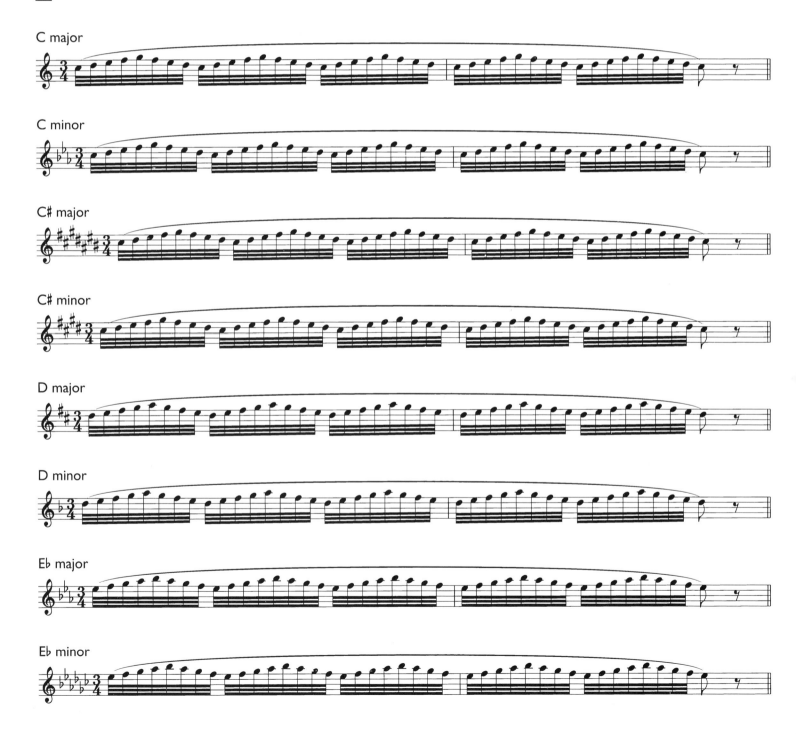

74

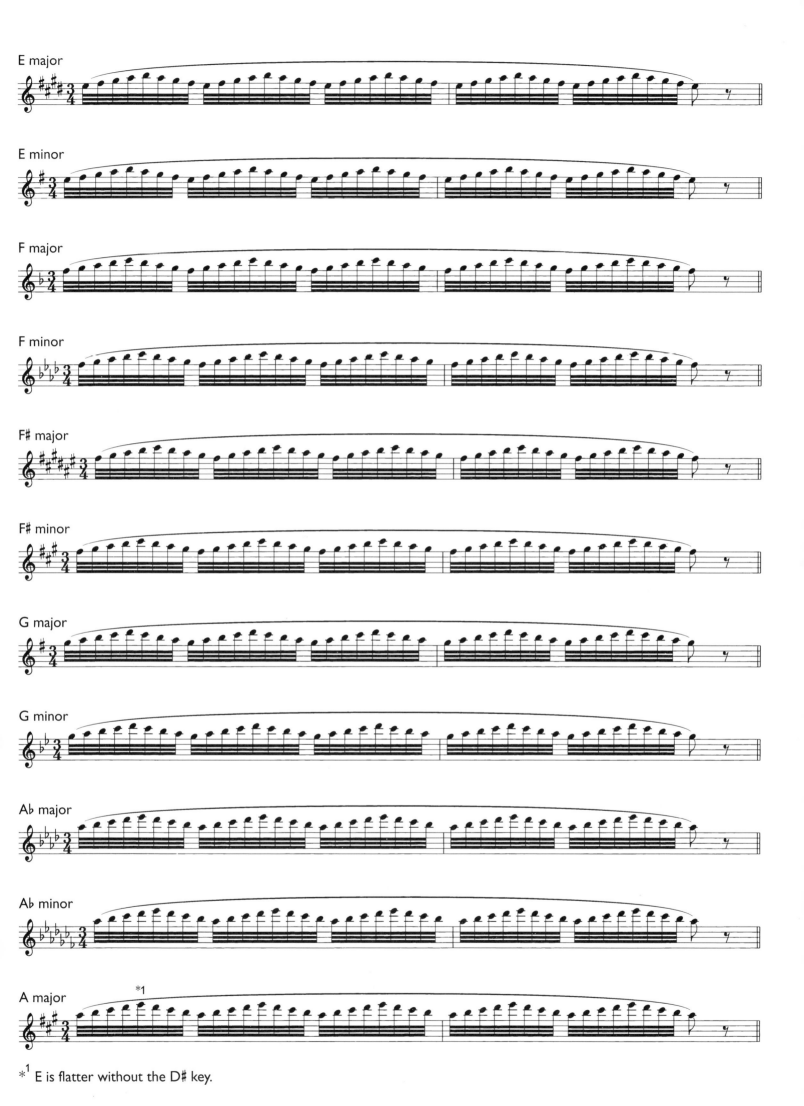

*¹ E is flatter without the D♯ key.

75

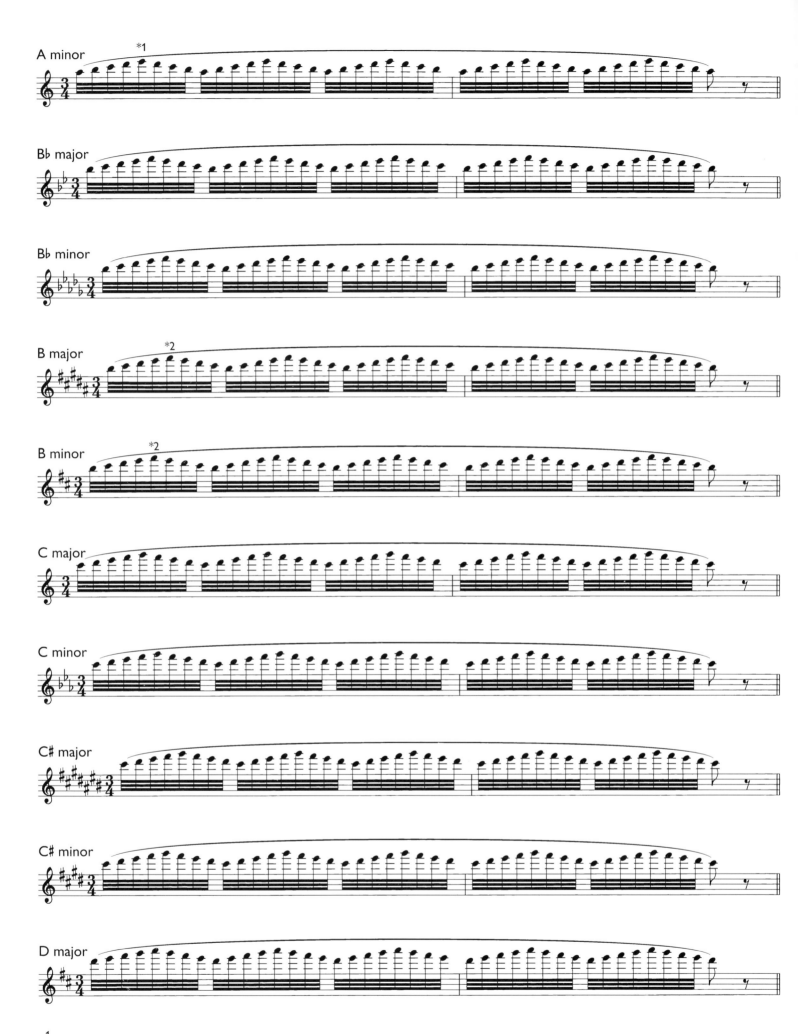

*¹ E is flatter without the D♯ key.

*² Why not alternate between the 2nd and 3rd fingers for F♯?

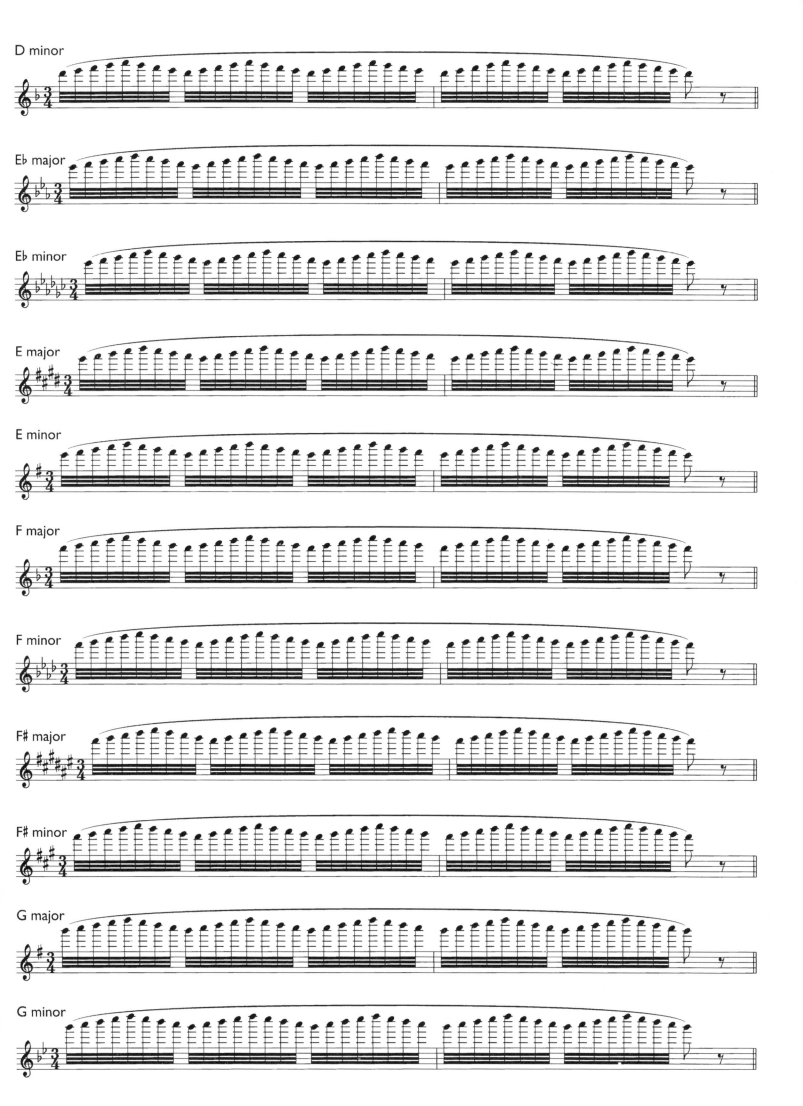

2 **Broken Scales 1**

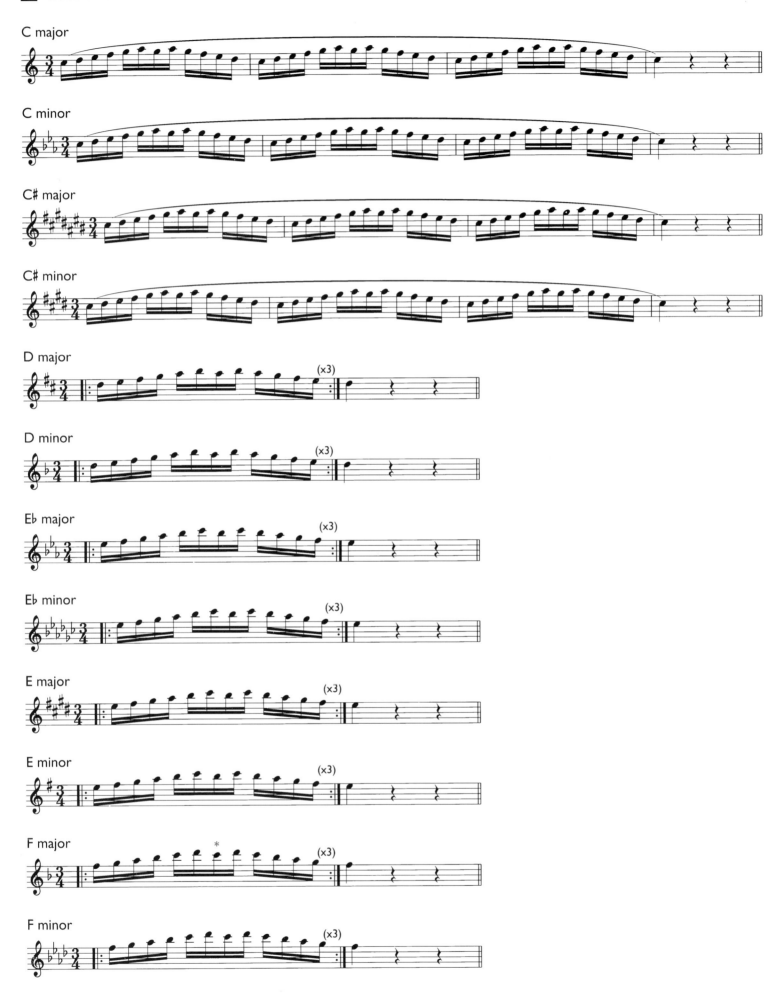

* Don't be tempted to use any but the normal fingering!

*1 Alternate between the 2nd and 3rd finger for F# in each repeat.

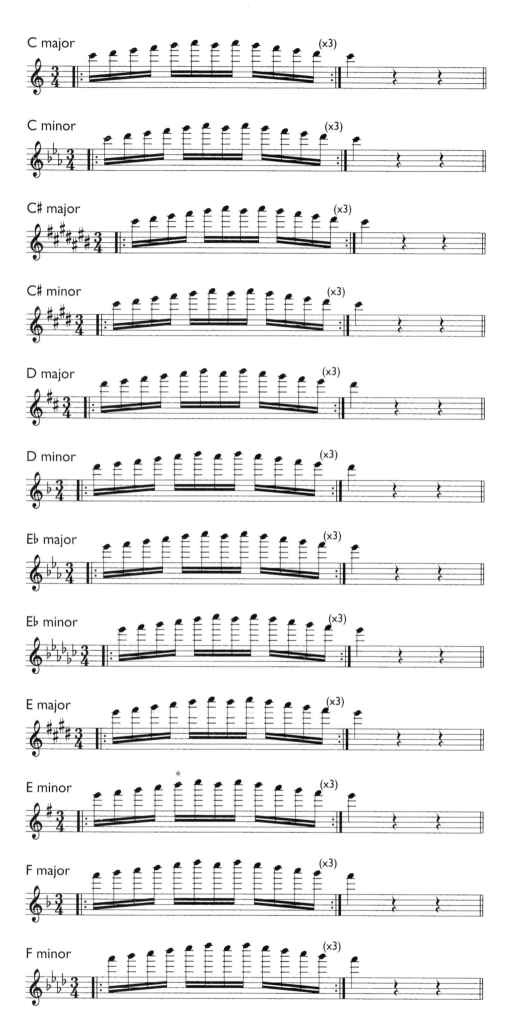

* Use usual B fingering, and remove the thumb for an easier, flatter C.
This is also useful in a fast chromatic scale to top C.

3 Broken Scales 2

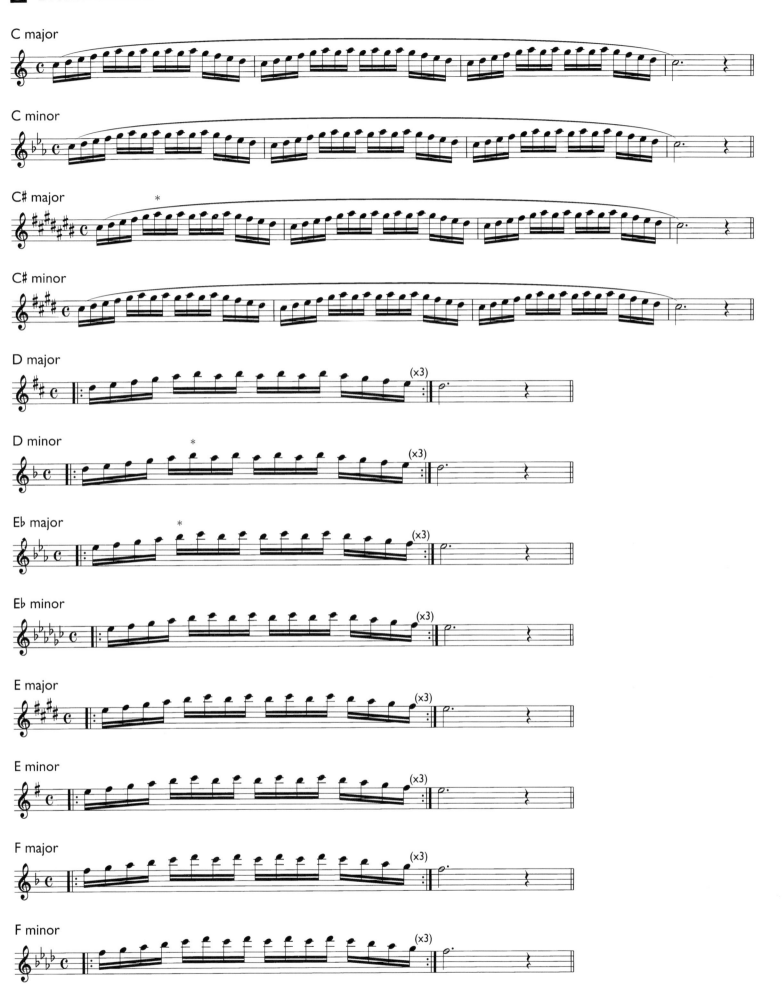

* Although difficult, it is more beneficial as an exercise, to use the 1st finger for A♯ or B♭ in the first two octaves throughout.

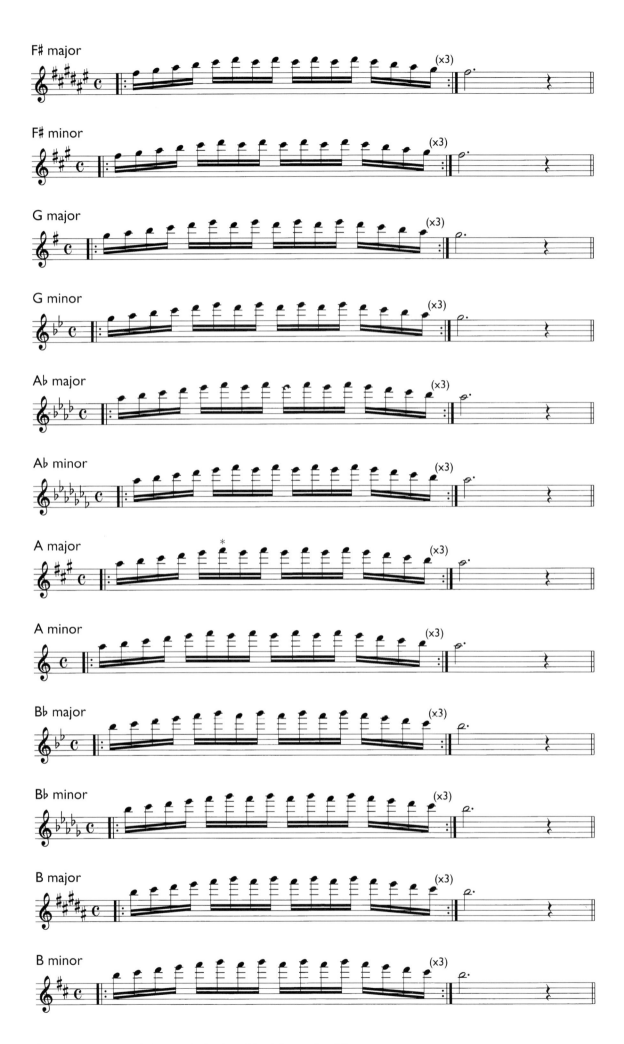

* Alternate in each bar with 2nd and 3rd finger for F#.

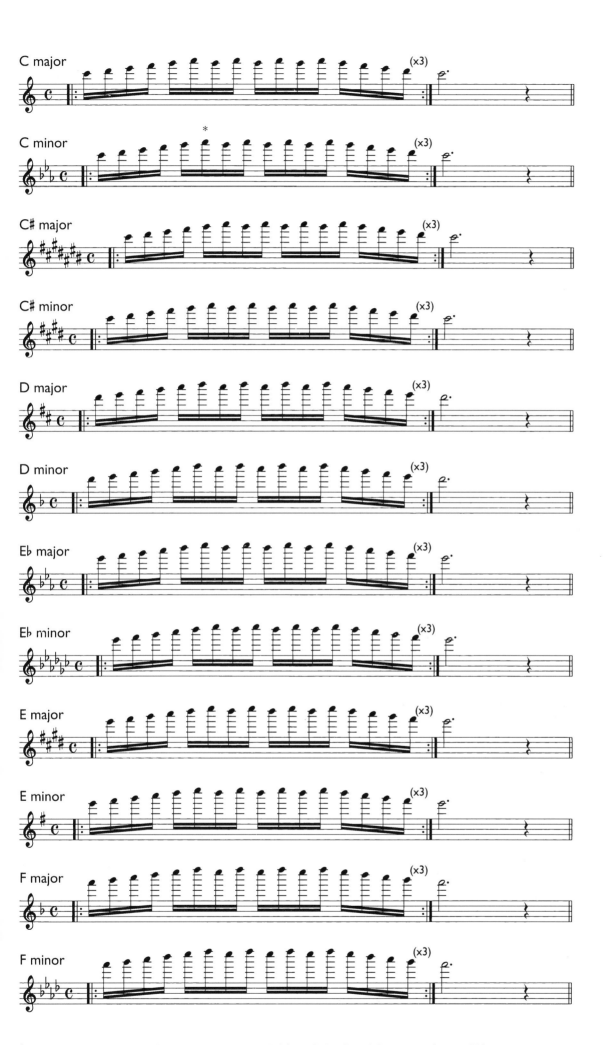

* Alternate in each bar between the normal A♭ and the 'long' fingering. (see p.33)

4 Thirds 1

84

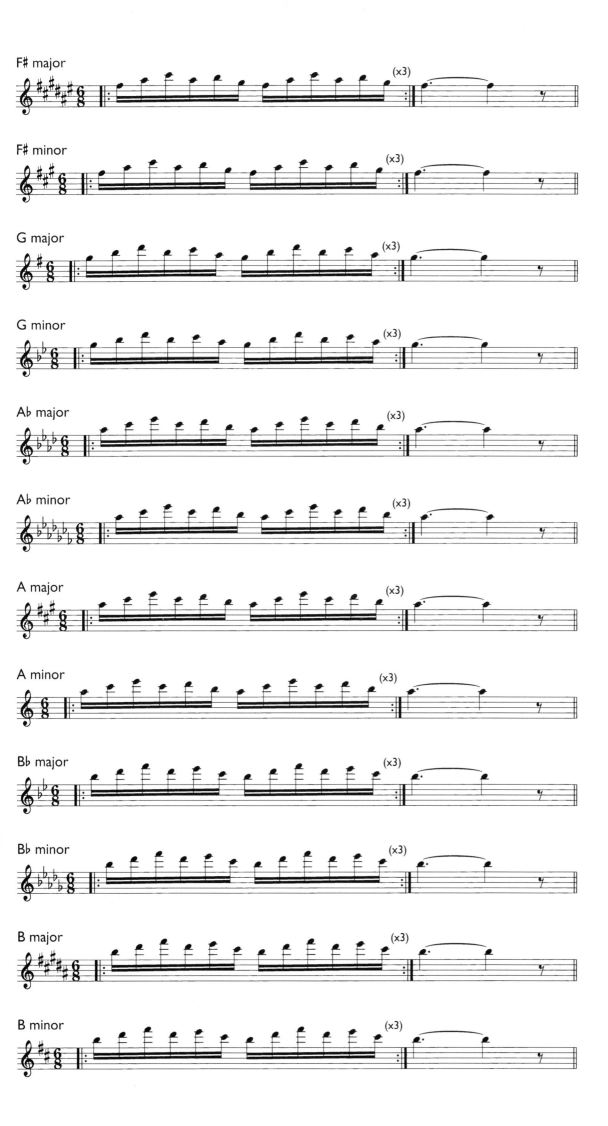

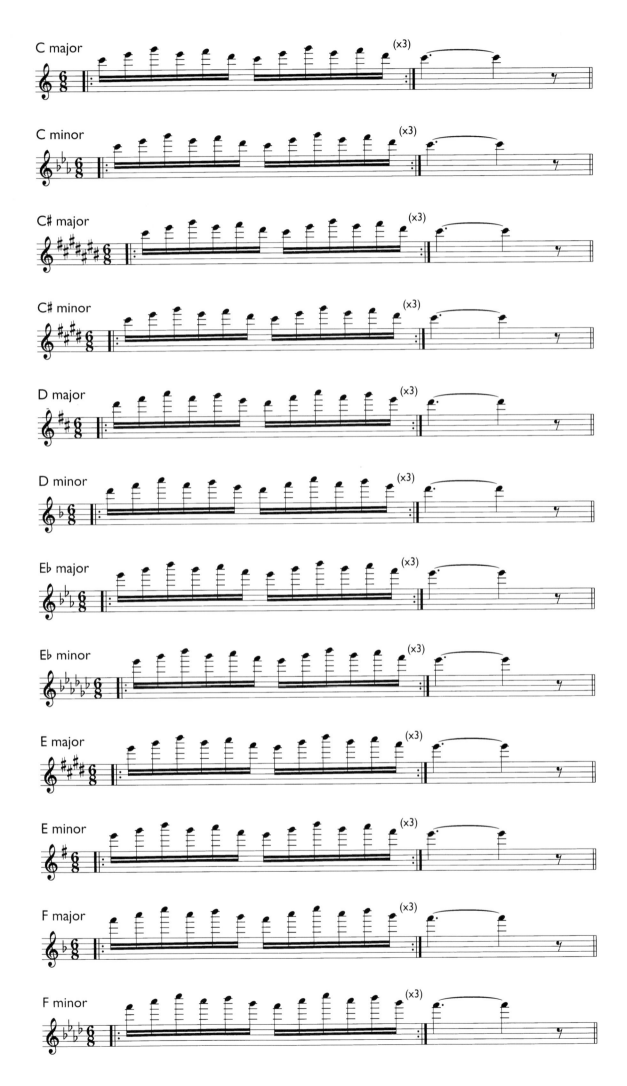

5 Thirds 2

The repetition of pairs of notes can lead us unthinkingly into bad habits: be sure that fingers aren't left down when they should be off. The differences in tone may not be so noticeable now but it will lead to further problems later.

6 Thirds 3

7 Chromatic

* To avoid 'cracking' of middle E♭ be sure the 1st finger of the left hand is off at the **start** of the note.

C major

C# major

D major

Eb major

E major

F major

8 FINAL STUDY

F major

F# major

G major

Ab major

A major

Bb major

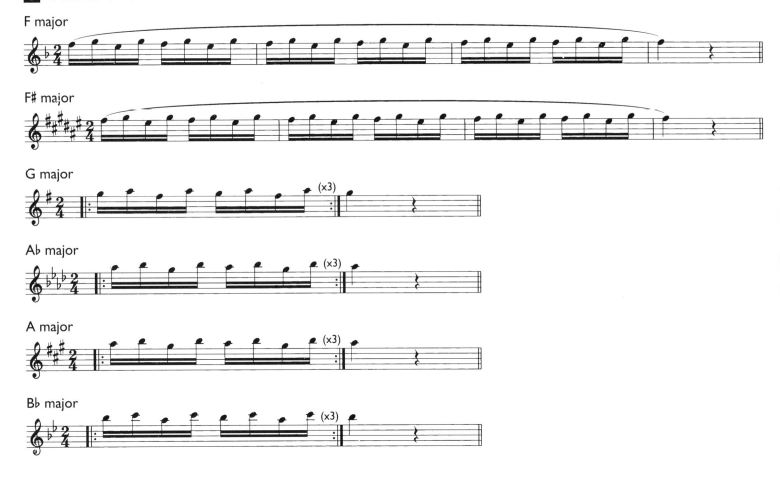

SECTION 6
Daily Exercises

This section contains the most popular daily exercises which are often used as 'warm-ups', tone exercises, and aids to better articulation. Most of them are commonly played from memory.

1

Refer to the Practice Card for articulation suggestions.

Trevor Wye

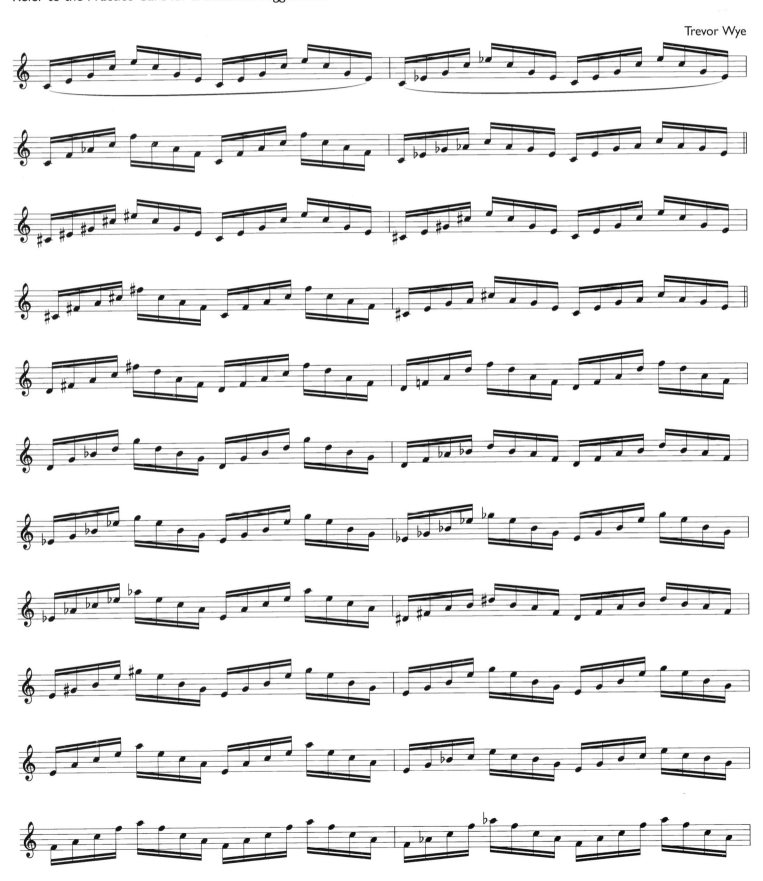

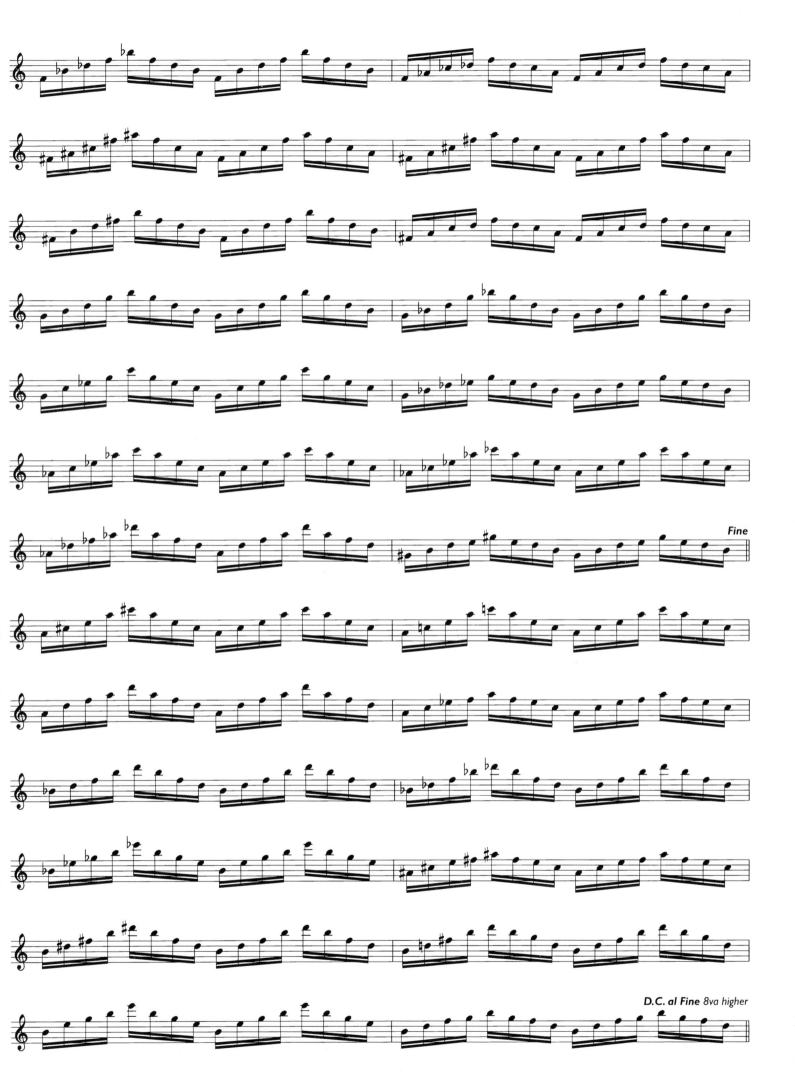

2

Refer to the Practice Card for articulation suggestions.

Trevor Wye

3

Refer to the Practice Card for articulation suggestions.

Trevor Wye

This can also be practised in the following ways:

4

Refer to the Practice Card for articulation suggestions.

Trevor Wye

This exercise can also be practised in the following forms:

5 No.2 from Twelve Studies (Boehm)

Practise in the following ways:

6 No.3 from Twelve Studies (Boehm)

7 No.4 from Twelve Studies (Boehm)

Refer to the Practice Card for articulation suggestions.

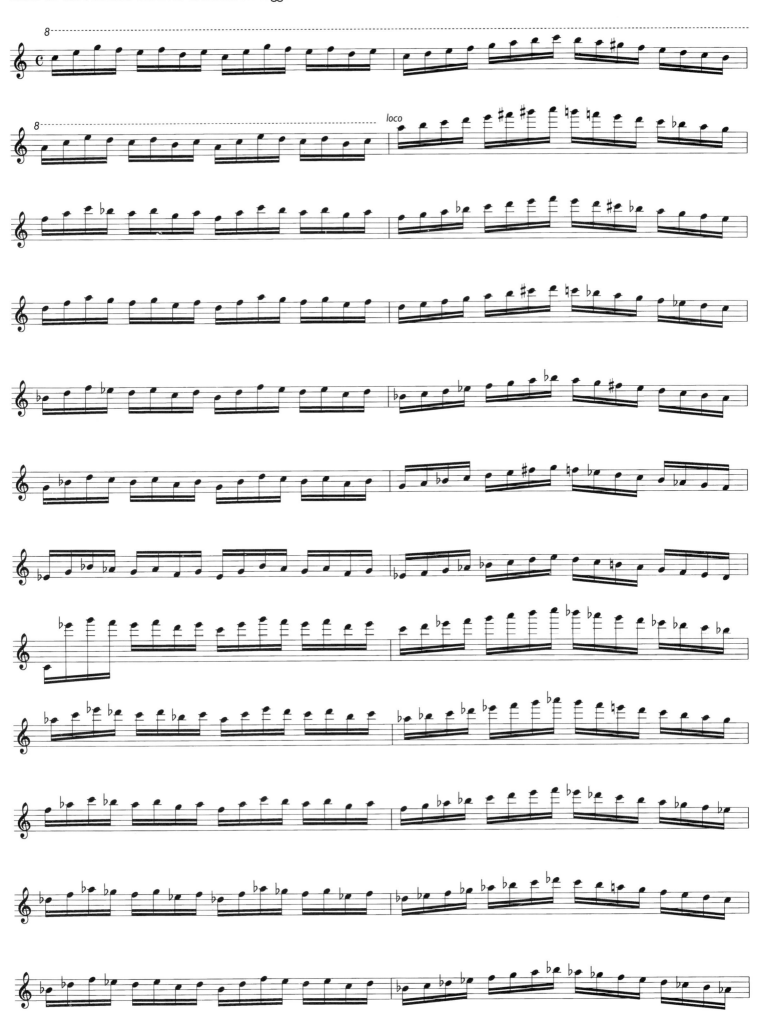

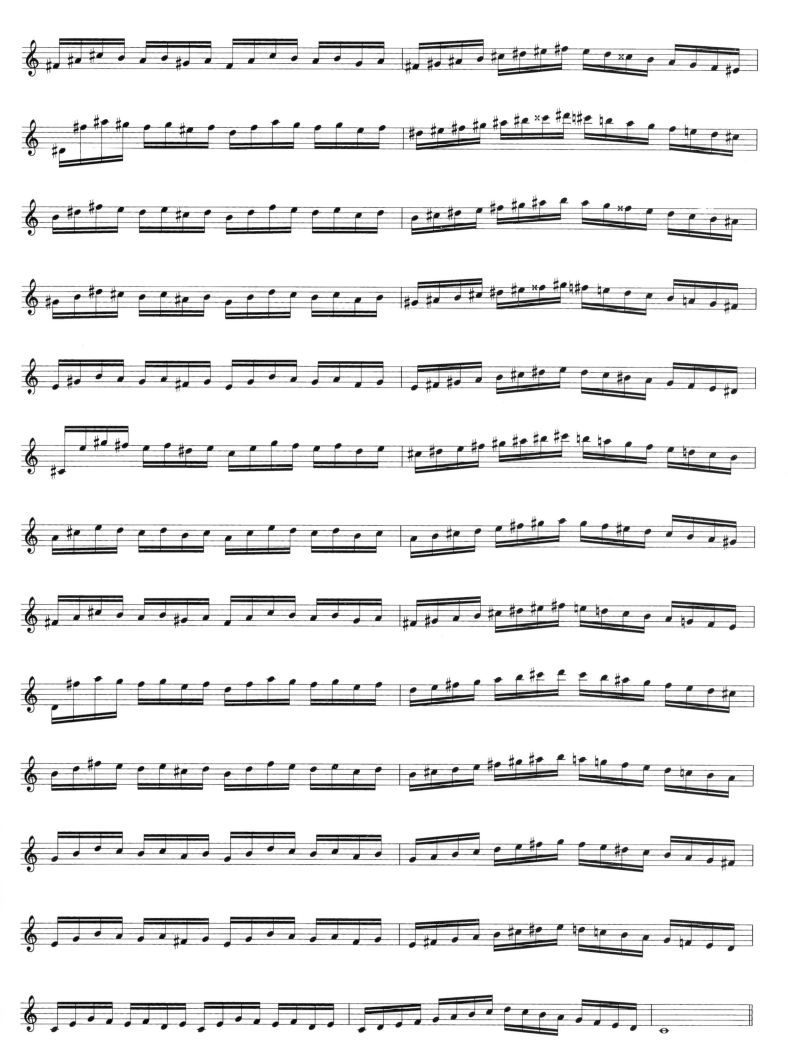

8 **No.9 from Twelve Studies (Boehm)**
Refer to the Practice Card for articulation suggestions.

No.12 from Twelve Studies (Boehm)

This may be practised in two ways:

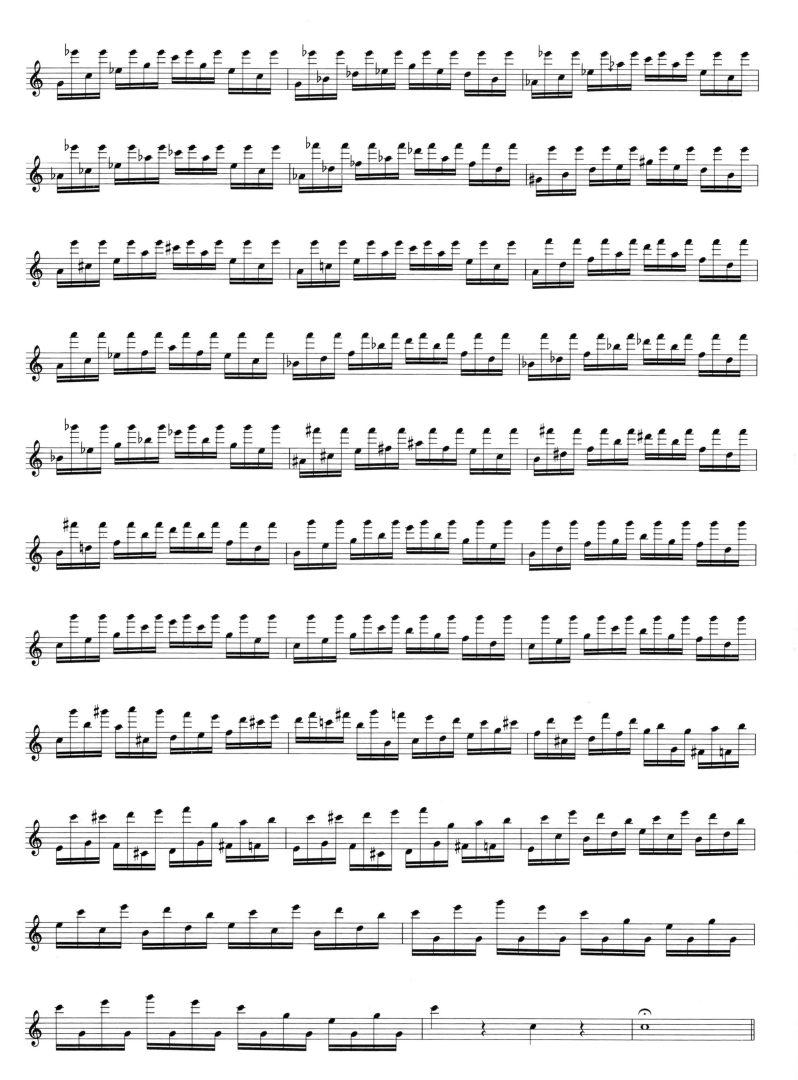

10 No.10 from Twelve Studies (Boehm)

This may be practised in two ways:

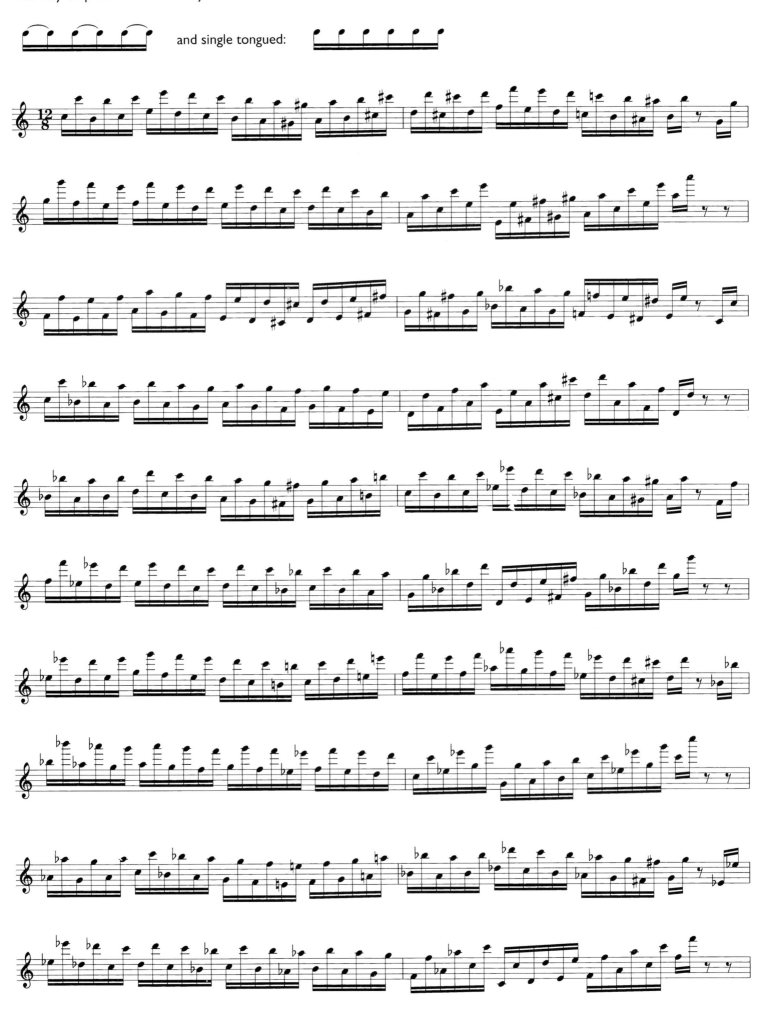

11 Right and Left Hand Co-ordination Exercise

Also practise in these keys:

and with the following articulation:

a) all slurred b) c) d) e)

and, when able, an octave higher.

* Don't forget the correct use of the D♯ key; it also helps the balance of the flute.

12 Four Studies on Perpetuum Mobile (Trevor Wye)

Original Solo

Practice in the following ways:

If this study is too difficult, begin by playing it in this pattern:

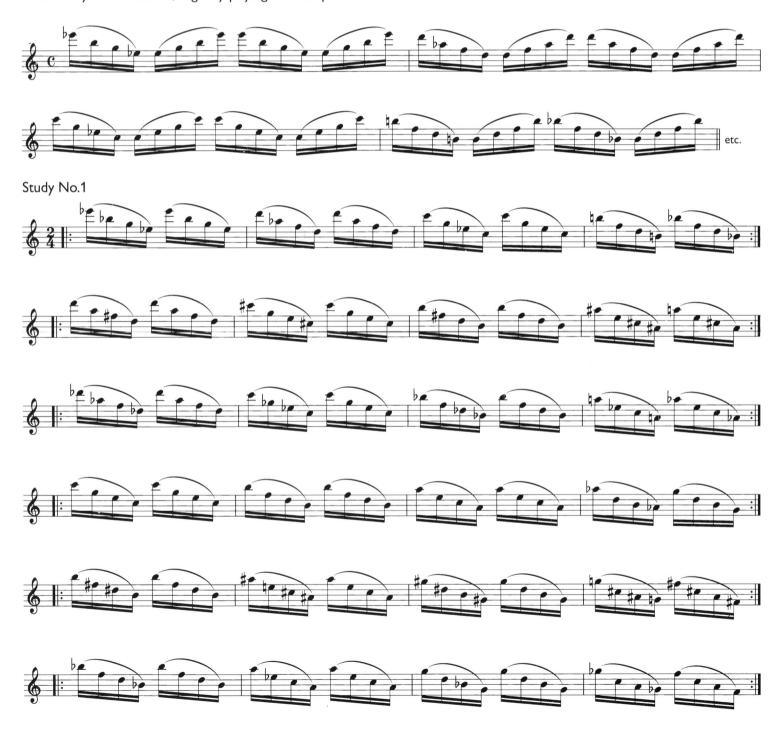

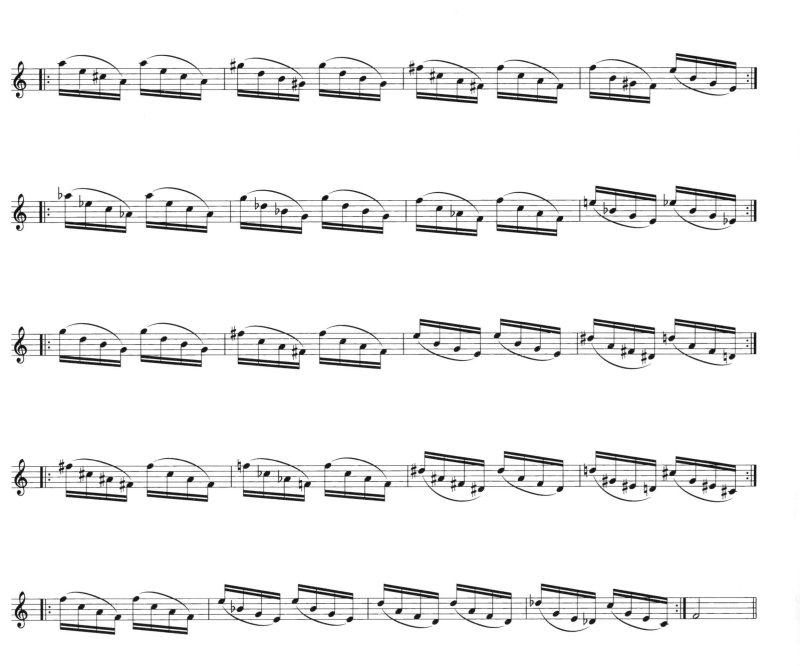

Study No.2
Practise also in the following ways:

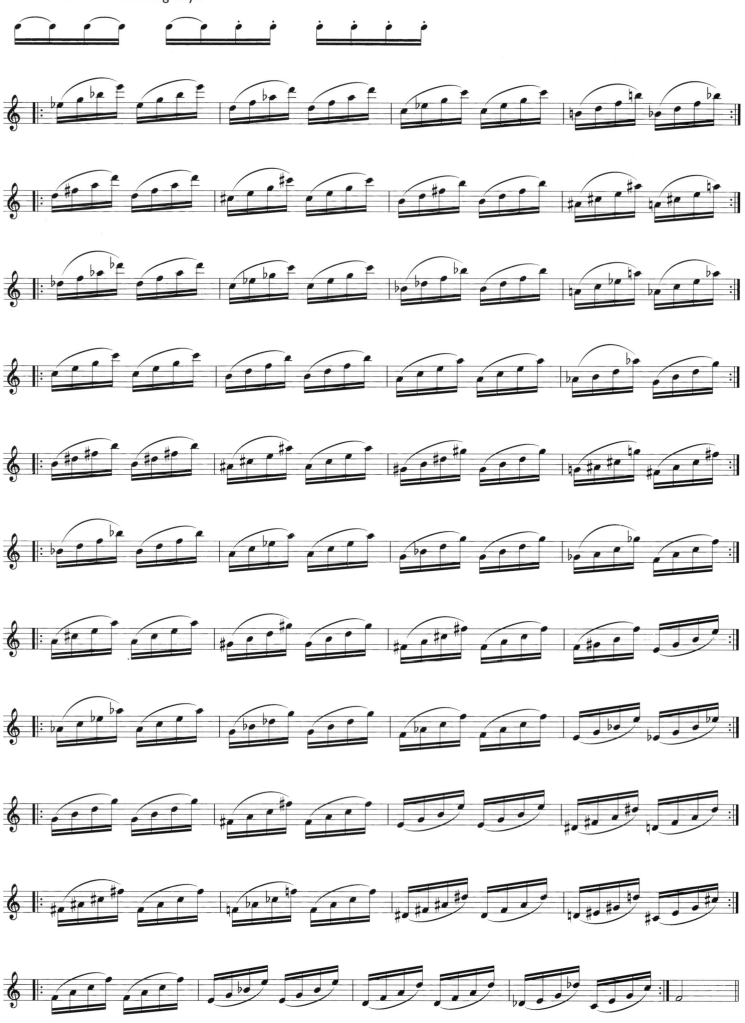

Study No.3
Practise also in the following ways:

a)   b)   c)   d)

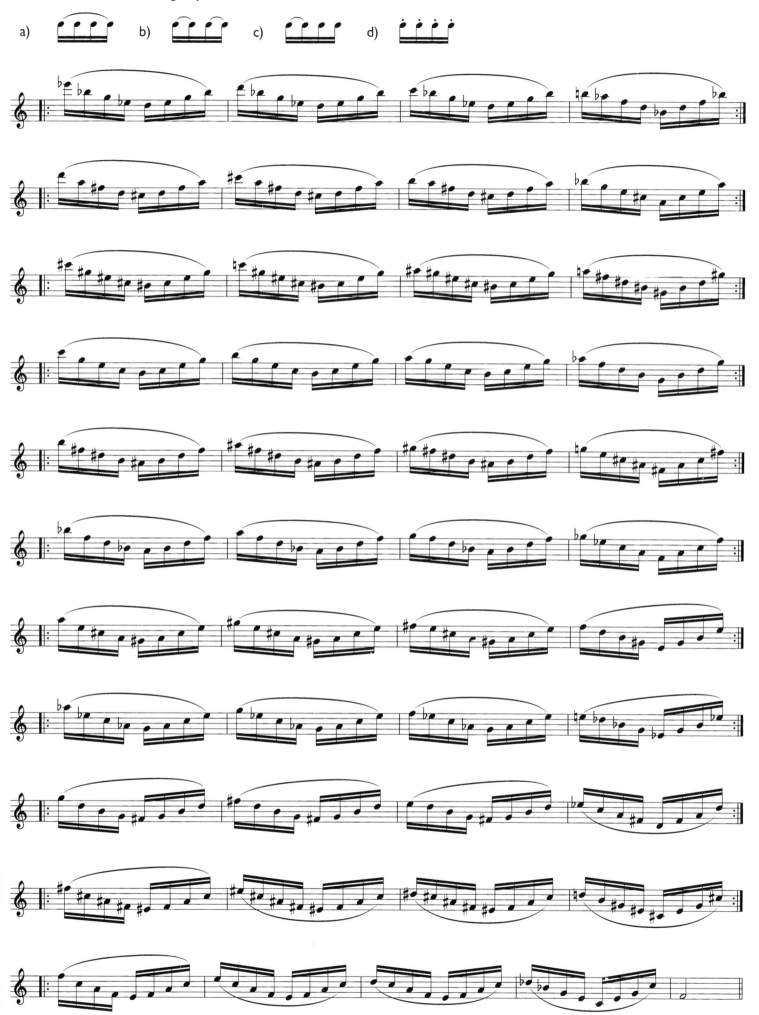

Study No.4

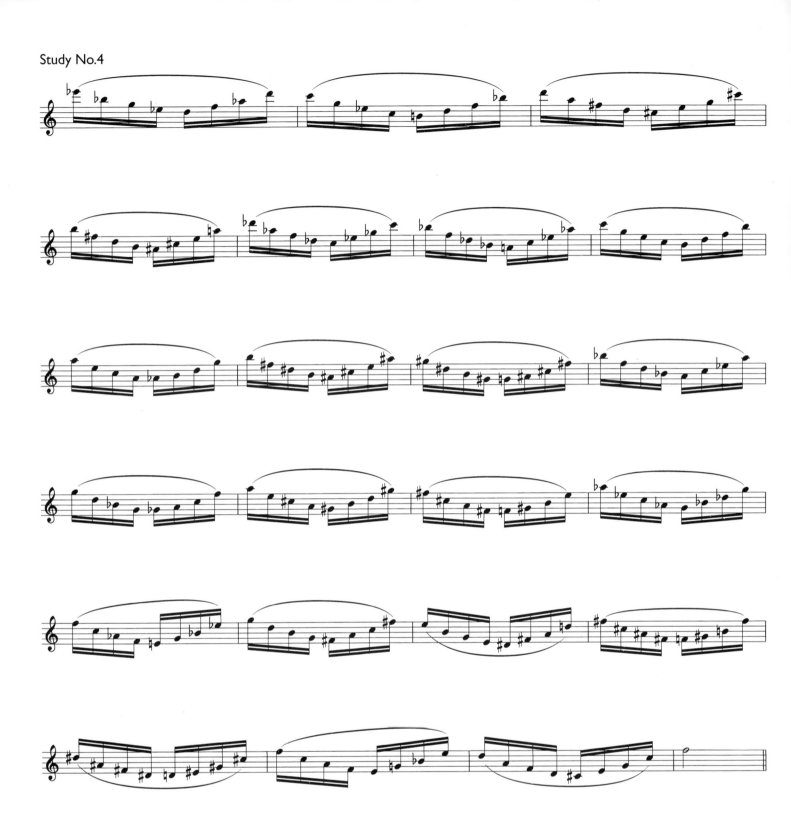

126

Practising

Here are some suggestions for varying the Reichert Exercise No.2 and the major and minor scale exercise p.52, and the scale exercises on p.23, two of the easiest exercises to memorise.

Essential books for all flautists from Novello.

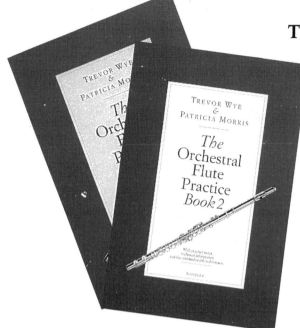

The Orchestral Flute Practice Books 1&2
Practice cadenzas, articulation, duets and trios, and learn about the fundamentals of orchestral writing and playing. Both books contain many pages of standard orchestral repertoire.

Bk.1 NOV120801 Bk.2 NOV120802

A Piccolo Practice Book
This book is now firmly established as the comprehensive collection of orchestral excerpts for students and professionals. An essential book for all piccolo player's libraries.

NOV120658

The Alto Flute Practice Book
This unique volume is the only comprehensive publication that covers all aspects of the alto flute, including a compendium of all the main orchestral extracts likely to be encountered by the working player.

NOV120781

Practice Books For The Flute (Omnibus Edition Books 1-5)
A bumper edition of Trevor Wye's famous practice books which concentrate on individual facets of flute playing in detail. This is an essential reference book to help conquer the technical difficulties of the instrument.

NOV120851